Teaming Rocks!

Collaborate in Powerful Ways
to Ensure Student Success

By Jill Spencer

National Middle School Association
Westerville, Ohio

Printed in the United States of America.

April Tibbles, Director of Publications
John Lounsbury, Editor, Professional Publications
Carla Weiland, Publications Editor
Cynthia Ritter, Designer
Dawn Williams, Publications Manager
Marcia Meade-Hurst, Senior Publications Representative
Derek Neal, Publications & Membership Marketing Manager

Library of Congress Cataloging-in-Publication Data

Spencer, Jill, 1946-
  Teaming rocks! : collaborate in powerful ways to ensure student success / Jill Spencer.
    p. cm.
  Includes bibliographical references.
  ISBN 978-1-56090-240-9
  1. Teaching teams--United States. 2. Middle school education--United States. I. Title.
  LB1029.T4S64 2010
  373.114'8--dc22
                            2010034233

National Middle School Association
4151 Executive Parkway, Suite 300
Westerville, Ohio 43081
1-800-528-NMSA   f: 614-895-4750
www.nmsa.org

Dedicated to

My sister, mentor, and friend,
Linn Spencer Hayes

Acknowledgements

As many writers before me have said, writing a book is never a solitary experience!

This book was inspired by my experiences with middle grades teams for over 35 years. The smart, dedicated, and compassionate educators I have been privileged to work with, observe, and connect with digitally here in Maine and across the country are too numerous to name for fear that I shall leave someone out. To all of you I say, "Thank you!"

Also, I would like to send a special thanks to several innovative educators who took time out of their busy schedules to share their ideas and experiences with me via Skype, e-mail, or iChat: Carol Duffy, Gert Nesin, Todd Williamson, Mark Springer, Wally Alexander, and Rick Wormeli. Their insights from their classrooms add richness to this book.

Nancy Rideout has been a friend since fifth grade. She is still teaching and keeps me firmly grounded in the realities of the classroom when I start to pontificate on what ought to be happening in schools. I appreciate her reality checks and regularly borrow ideas from her for my writing and presentations.

The possibilities for technology integration grow at a rapid pace. Three people—Barbara Greenstone, Lisa Hogan, and Chris Toy— keep me current. They respond to my urgent late night instant messages when I can't get a program to work and share their latest digital exploits that keep me experimenting and learning.

Nancy Doda wrote the wonderful Foreword for *Teaming Rocks!* She was the middle level speaker my colleagues and I were in awe of when we attended conferences and institutes. Over the years Nancy has become a friend, but I am still in awe. Her knowledge of how kids learn and passion for middle level education still inspire me to work harder and learn more. Nancy's writing the Foreword is an incredible honor.

And finally, thank you to my editors who make revision and editing fun. John Lounsbury and Carla Weiland from NMSA have been wonderful editors with which to work. Their questions, probing, and suggestions make *Teaming Rocks!* more readable and help me to continue to develop my skills as a writer—a never-ending process.

Table of Contents

Foreword

Teaming for Phenomenal Learning: What We Have Been Waiting for

Teaching teams have been the hallmark of the modern middle school. Over more than three decades, effective teams have been associated with increased personalization, reduction in bullying, improved job satisfaction, a reduction in school discipline problems, superior parent involvement, and significantly improved student learning. In spite of supportive research data and widely successful practice, school districts are struggling to maintain teaching teams in their middle schools. This struggle is in part the consequence of a long-standing misunderstanding of teaming's ultimate purposes. Organizing interdisciplinary teaching teams has always been about advancing powerful student learning yet many middle schools missed that mark. Some principals observe, as Jill writes, that their teams never fully utilized teaming's potential and simply spend too little time on curriculum and instruction. Teachers working on teams likewise confess that beyond talking about students, they have yet to develop a solid set of competencies in managing team curriculum and instruction. Many more teams find that dream deferred as team planning time and support are severely limited. Ultimately in a time of bare bones budgets, districts are wondering if the expense of organized interdisciplinary teams is warranted, particularly as they focus nearly exclusively on standardized test results. Teaming is no doubt at a vulnerable crossroad.

Thankfully Jill's book, *Teaming Rocks!*, arrives just in the nick of time. Here is a resource that will help teachers across the Unites States and beyond resurrect the power and promise of teaming. Each chapter is packed with practical tools and wisdom to advance the work of teaching teams. From building a team community to addressing diverse student needs, integrating literacy across the curriculum, and advancing students research and inquiry skills, Jill helps us leap right over the steady stuff we already do well into the kind of teaming that will yield the greatest results for student learning and success. Moreover, Jill makes us feel right at home and shelters us to take worthy risks. Weaving together vivid vignettes and manageable methods, Jill makes us feel like she is sitting right next to us on some old sofa in the teacher's lounge, chatting us through the hefty work of effective teaming.

Unique in many ways, this book is the first of its kind to make explicit the oft-cited, but weakly acknowledged truth that teaming is about advancing student learning—21st century student learning to be precise. Jill's rich experience with the Maine Learning Technology Initiative and classroom use of technology provide us with a comprehensive collection of Web resources and technology tools that will no doubt be new to most of us, with the possible exception of the technology expert in your school. What's most exciting though is that Jill doesn't bury us in a plethora of Web sites. She has done the hard work of sorting out what works and then providing us with many contextualized examples that help us imagine how we might put these resources to work.

Learning that is future savvy not only embraces technology; it embraces the broader, bolder agenda of raising a generation of thoughtful, socially conscious citizens who use knowledge to improve their own lives and the world. Jill brings us back to this most ambitious and progressive agenda—the middle school curriculum. In one very vibrant chapter, she reminds us that a teaching team offers us an opportunity to pursue curriculum integration where teachers and students co-create units of study that honor not only the standards to be taught, but the questions and issues that are personally and socially significant to all members of the team community. In this way, as Jill's examples verify, students live out the democratic way of life and begin to see themselves as responsible members of a team and ultimately of the world.

For those who have always thought the work of integrating the curriculum was out of reach, this chapter will shore you up. Jill provides us with such varied examples of how teachers have done this work and such helpful guidance on how to do it gracefully that teams at all levels of readiness can dig in. Most importantly, Jill acknowledges with the mind of a fellow teacher, the challenges and successes of others who have ventured to do this important work.

Teaming Rocks! is a wonderful and needed contribution to our collection of books on teaming. It challenges us to frame the teaming opportunity in terms of student academic success without ever ignoring the needs of the young adolescent learner. You simply cannot read this book and think teaming fails to address the very critical contemporary focus on student learning. As you consider readings suited for your back home professional learning communities, *Teaming Rocks!* would be a wise choice. That is because this book is particularly well suited for the "read, try, and reflect" approach associated with meaningful professional development. Jill invites us into that kind of work as she steadily pulls us into our classrooms and into our most reflective teaching selves with her poignant examples, questions and insights.

However you read it, alone, with your team, or with others with whom you work, you will use it and surely be better equipped to make your own team one that offers young adolescents the support, belonging, stimulation, and personalization they so need and deserve.

Nancy Doda
August, 2010

Jill Invites You to Take a Look Back—and Find a Way Forward

"Can you teach math?" I must have hesitated because the principal then asked me if I could balance my checkbook. There were low expectations for math teachers in 1973! I was not going to admit that reconciling my bank statement with my checkbook was a very low priority, so I said *yes*! I looked around the table at the other 11 people (There really were a dozen educators present) quizzing me on why I thought I should be their choice for the eighth grade social studies position. "What was I thinking?" kept bouncing around inside my brain as I looked from face to face. Although I knew very little about teaching, I had enjoyed my time in another middle school as the ed tech running the library. "How hard could it be to teach social studies? I knew a lot about the subject," I had mused when filling out the application. Going to the interview, I had expected to meet with the principal, not all of the teams looking for new teachers, so I left the interview in a bit of a daze. However, that night the phone call came—I was hired!

That phone call planted the seed that grew into the passion I developed for middle grades teaming. I understood the concept of making a large school more intimate by organizing students into smaller groups. After all, the 3000-student high school I graduated from had been broken up into houses, and I had been in Barry House in Building 1. I had Mr. Peterson for homeroom all three years, and for two years Mr. Rosen was my math teacher and Mr. Warshaw, my English teacher. Was Newton High School looping in 1962? I don't know, but I do know that being part of a smaller community certainly helped me feel connected and less overwhelmed. Therefore, I was primed to be part of Team 8B and embark on what proved to be a grand educational adventure. We taught integrated units, team-taught lessons, flexed the schedule, grouped and regrouped students, integrated field trips into the curriculum, and really knew and enjoyed our students. I learned something new every day about teaching from my teammates. Common planning time was energizing as we crafted units and brainstormed ways to engage our students in learning. These early years convinced me that teaming was without a doubt the most effective way to meet young adolescents' learning needs.

When a new principal came onboard with an organizational vision that encompassed only departments for grades 7–12 and not teaming for the middle grades, my seventh and eighth grade colleagues and I were crushed. Students began to fall through the proverbial cracks and got into trouble. It was now nearly impossible to maintain continuous communication about specific students because the only time we met was in the guidance office to address specific issues. We kept trying to recapture the essence of teaming by working with other grade level teachers in our subject areas. We did some neat things, but those few activities could not replace the benefits that came from common planning time with others who share the same group of students. When we changed principals once again and teams were reinstituted, my colleagues and I were thrilled.

Recently one of my teammates from those glory days asked me if middle level education were dead. He reported that in his school common planning time was greatly diminished and was spent in PET meetings and parent conferences. His team never planned curriculum together and rarely shared insights about student strengths and weaknesses. His story is just one of many such stories that I hear as I travel across the country consulting with schools. It feels like mass amnesia has taken hold, and the good reasons why schools for young adolescents were organized into teams in the first place have been forgotten. We often seem to completely ignore the research that shows students in schools that implemented the middle school concept and followed the recommendations in *Turning*

Points (teaming, heterogeneous grouping, common planning time at least four times a week, advisory, challenging curriculum, and developmentally appropriate instruction) achieve at higher levels than students in schools without these conditions.

Particularly disturbing is that fewer and fewer middle grades teams are using whatever common planning time they still have to collaborate and devise ways to effectively apply best practice and research to benefit their students. Under the gun of "accountability as measured by test scores" I believe too many schools have given up on teaming even though it is the best way to achieve those mandated scores and also meet additional goals currently being neglected.

This diminished vision of teaming directly affects students in many ways. Instead of intellectually stimulating curriculum that teaches skills in authentic contexts, teams are following scripted instruction. With layer upon layer of programs deemed to be "teacher proof" and the proverbial panaceas for learning problems moved into place, no longer does an energized teaching faculty act in innovative ways to solve these problems. Alas, too many schools and districts have lost sight of the fact that teams are on the ground floor with their students and have the opportunity to size up their needs and respond in a timely fashion. What really distresses me is that this turning away from true teaming comes now when teams have the potential to be even more effective than in the past. They can apply knowledge about brain development and its processes that didn't exist 30 years ago to their instructional practices and take advantage of the flexibility and endless resources that new technology devices and the Internet provide. Too many middle schools are not taking advantage of the potential of teams to meet students' learning needs through the combined power of technology tools and new learning research.

A curriculum coordinator recently told me about her perception that teachers talk about common planning time in ways that benefit only them; she didn't hear them say anything about the benefits for students. That perception was one reason for her recommendation that teams be disbanded. I wanted to cry. So that very day I decided to write this book. I wanted to help unleash the hidden potential that resides in teams who are committed to making sure each and every one of their students soars to academic and personal heights. My purpose is not to explain how or why to establish teams. Many fine books such as *Implementing and Improving Teaming: A Handbook for Middle Level Leaders, We Gain More Than We Give: Teaming in Middle Schools, and WOW What A Team!* already fulfill that purpose. *Teaming Rocks! Collaborate in Powerful Ways to Ensure Student Success* is for existing teams who are ready to explore ways to collaborate more fully in building the skills and confidence students need to succeed in later education and life.

Writing this book in an informal, personal style as a classroom teacher, I hope to contribute to what I envision as the renaissance of middle grades teaming. I want to see teaming not just return to the practices of the past before they were dismantled by high stakes testing, teacher-proof curriculum, and punitive measures for underachieving middle schools, but to evolve to an even higher level of effectiveness that is reflective of current research, technology, and current challenges. Teaming is the proven vehicle for carrying out an intellectually stimulating 21st century curriculum that incorporates literacy, numeracy, digital fluency, critical and creative thinking, all of which are possible when a team of teachers collaborate as true professionals.

The reader will notice that I make some assumptions about existing teams. I write as if teams have four teachers, each responsible for a specific curriculum area, as they most commonly are, and that they have some common planning time. Of course there are wonderful teams across the world that are organized differently, including those that teach in a totally integrated fashion, and regrettably, there are still some with virtually no common planning time. I suggest, too, that advisory is a possible time for implementing several proposed ideas although not all teams have a formal advisory. Middle school teachers who have to live by the notion of flexibility will not have difficulty figuring out how they can apply ideas from *Teaming Rocks!* to their own situations.

I hope this book sparks spirited discussions within middle grades schools and that teams assess where they are as a collaborative teaching team and adapt some of my ideas and strategies. I believe it is important to build effective, strong teams that continuously strive to improve their practice. However, I want to stress that I'm not offering a recipe or a checklist for what teams should do. Each school's situation is unique, and the teams within the school must consider and reflect on their students' needs and take appropriate steps to continue to move forward. It is important work because teams save students' lives and inspire young adolescents to learn, achieve, and follow their dreams. It is my fervent wish that *Teaming Rocks!* be simply a small contributor to discussions and actions that will make teaming what it should be, can be, and what it always has been, the heart and soul of the middle school. *Let's Rock!*

1

Become a Team That Inspires Your Students

Teams have the power to create an environment that motivates students to soar academically and personally. Effective teaming takes time and effort, but the rewards for both students and teachers are immeasurable.

Reaching the Heights

The drizzle stopped as the school buses pulled in the parking lot for the Precipice Trail that snaked its way up the east side of Champlain Mountain in Acadia National Park. Shifting their daypacks and pulling off rain gear they would leave behind, eighty eighth graders tumbled out of the buses. Craning their necks, they stared up at the mountain. "Are we really going up there?" whispered Jillian. "I'm worried about having to creep along that narrow trail that we've heard about."

Jillian was not particularly athletic but felt comfortable sharing her fears because the team had developed such an esprit de corps and "can do" attitude over the year. She and her classmates had worked together on a variety of projects and learned to push themselves. With support from both her teachers and her classmates, Jillian had taken on roles she never had thought she was capable of—including organizing a field trip for her class to a local organic farm to study sustainable agriculture. She also had performed her own original poetry for a class podcast. She thought to herself, "How much scarier can it be to climb a mountain than to read your own poem into a microphone that will allow anyone in the whole wide world to hear it?"

Seven hundred feet up the 1000-foot seemingly vertical trail had Jillian rethinking her prior bravado. The trail was slippery from the morning drizzle, very narrow, and seemed to drop off into nothing. She hesitated as she approached a curve in the trail where she knew she had to hug the cliff to get around the curve. Dan encouraged her from behind, "Just don't look down and you'll be all right." Of course, she looked down and then swallowed hard. She began to edge further up and around the twist in the trail. Her best friend, Libby, was urging her on from just ahead. "There." She had made it and sighed as her heart beat rapidly.

The group continued climbing until all had reached the summit. With a sense of satisfaction and pride, they looked out over Mt. Desert Island and Frenchman's Bay. Everyone had made it to the top together. This outing was the culmination of their eighth grade year celebrating not only the completion of the rigorous Maine Studies semester, but also the students' growth as individuals able to face all types of challenges and as a cohesive team that had learned the value of collaboration and respect.

Over and over the stories one reads of individuals who have succeeded are highlighted by the role of mentors, support systems, and special experiences that inspired these individuals to make life-altering decisions. Middle grades teams are in the perfect position to provide meaningful experiences that will shape their students' lives in significant ways. Working together as a team committed to crafting inspirational and meaningful learning experiences for their students provides teachers with a sense of professional accomplishment. Also, parents are pleased when their children respond positively to their school experiences during the often-turbulent adolescent years.

Create extraordinary learning environments for students because:

- **The middle grades are particularly vulnerable times for students as they undergo extensive changes and make decisions that will affect their emotional and physical health as well as their education and career options as adults.** "Young people undergo more rapid and profound personal changes between the ages of 10 and 15 than at any other time in their lives" (NMSA, 2010, p.5). Young adolescents are both a challenging and exhilarating group of youngsters to teach. Educators need innovative thinking, patience, flexibility, and a solid grounding in pedagogy and curriculum to address the learning needs of this often-at-risk age group. It is an ethical and economic imperative that students leave middle school

3

with the competence and confidence they need to face their next set of challenges. Students' achievements and behaviors formed in the middle grades strongly influence their college and career readiness as well as the probability of their dropping out of school (ACT, Balfanz). Teams that share ideas and work collaboratively are in the best position to build intellectually stimulating learning environments while responding to the varied social and psychological needs of their students. Teams that inspire their students to stretch beyond their expectations as Christa McAuliffe, the first teacher in space, said, *"touch the future."*

- **A smoothly working team is efficient and effective. In both the business world and in education, teaming increases productivity and effectiveness.** New and improved products, time used more efficiently, increased sales, and contented work forces are among the benefits of teaming in the corporate world (Hoerr). In education, productivity translates into increased achievement, more contact with parents, and varied learning experiences that meet the diverse needs of students. Teachers in teams share information and respond quickly to individual student's problems. The multiple perspectives of the teachers on a team lead to many creative and innovative ways to engage students in curriculum. Being part of a well-functioning team is not only professionally satisfying, but also makes for a fun work environment. The enthusiasm emanating from the teachers translates into a positive and energetic response from the students.

- **Teaming provides teachers with the support, inspiration, and opportunity for creative problem solving that make teaching so rewarding.** One in five teachers leaves education within three years. Reasons given include discipline issues, substandard working conditions, and a sense of isolation and frustration. Teaming is the *fabulous* antidote to such conditions. Behavior is not a problem when there is a team to support one another. Working conditions are not dismal when there is friendly support at hand, and enthusiasm grows rather than shrivels when teammates jump in with both feet to support an activity or event. Teaming helps individual teachers bring to fruition their calling and to know that they are, indeed, making a difference in the lives of their students.

Teaming, then, is a research-based organizational strategy that enables teachers to provide the cognitive, social, and psychological support necessary for young adolescents to develop a love of learning, respect for self and others, and effectively meets stated achievement goals. Young adolescents need to be a part of such a learning community as they are bombarded daily with conflicting messages and need help in sorting through the issues they face. Today's educators face a major dilemma because their students need a more complete education than past generations have required while enticing influences tug their students in other directions. In addition the mass media and music industry rarely extol the virtues of education. Teachers today confront immense challenges as they develop and execute units that must not only teach skills and impart information, but also offer guidance in maturing students' social, emotional, and moral development.

Two Ways to Go About Building a More Effective Team

1 **Take time to work your way through the process of becoming a really effective team.** Two to five individual teachers who share the same group of students do not automatically function in concert as a team. Becoming a real team is an evolutionary process that requires dialogue and conversations, sometimes spirited conversations. In teams of four or five these conversations are likely to be rather extensive. In the business world the development of teams is supported with both financial and human resources. Google "team building" and a multitude of sites advertising services come up. Most of these organizations are not targeting schools because schools lack the money to hire such specialized consultants. If a middle grades team wishes to become exceptional, its members are going to have to invest their own time and energy to achieve this goal. A cookout in a team member's backyard before school starts is a perfect setting to begin the conversation. It's off campus so there is no pull to go to individual rooms and set up for the first day of school, nor is there an intercom to interrupt. Teams can focus on building relationships, a common vision, and a plan of action that will provide the best working conditions possible for students and for themselves. A few summer hours will smooth the way for operations in the fall. If a team is responsive to students and parents, inspires students to give extra effort, and envisions their role as integral to student cognitive and personal development, all parties will benefit. In exceptional teams, members also stretch one another. Skills and understandings will develop that will open unexpected professional doors in the future. Institutionally, a school with exceptional teams builds community support that will be reflected at budget time.

There are many ways to develop a sense of team. Again, Google "team building" and several sites come up with information about team building. A closer-to-home suggestion is to check out the professional development section in your school library. There are probably one or two books on middle school team development that are full of good advice and strategies for building effective teams. Two excellent titles that you should secure are:

> *We Gain More Than We Give: Teaming in Middle Schools.* This National Middle School Association (NMSA) publication is the most comprehensive treatment of teaming available. A classic, it presents history, research, best practice, strategies, and examples of teams in action.

> *Camel-Makers: Building Effective Teacher Teams Together.* This NMSA book addresses the "gut" issues of teaming in a most engaging and enlightening way.

Check out other books and media resources on teaming at www.nmsa.org

A critical element of teaming is to have appropriate conversations every time there is a change of personnel on the team, even if it's just one person. Any change means a change in team dynamics. When there is no induction for a new teammate, the newcomer figuring out the team procedures and processes on her own usually makes a miscalculation or misinterpretation, and tensions arise. Be sensitive to teammates' feelings and hesitations. Disintegrating team dynamics easily foil the potential for team magic. Be proactive as a team and renew conversations about how the team is regularly operating.

2 **Define what you stand for as a team.** When reading about teams that have inspired their students, you will notice in such instances it is always obvious that these teams' thinking transcends subject matter. There is an organizing principle or umbrella vision that drives their work.

- In *The Story of Alpha: A Multiage, Student-Centered Team— 33 Years and Counting* by Susan Kuntz, teachers reported they "were always on a mission." It was defined by a commitment to an activity-centered developmental approach to teaching and learning.

- At Warsaw Middle School in Pittsfield, Maine, the entire school practices the FISH philosophy: Be There, Play, Make Their Day, and Choose Your Attitude (www.charthouse.com/content.aspx?name=home2).

- Ross Burkhardt in *Inventing Powerful Pedagogy* describes how he and his teammate Cliff Lennon developed a set of attributes they called Distinctions *(acknowledgement, appreciation, commitment, communication, cooperation, respect, responsibility, risk, and trust)* that served as guiding principles for working with their students.

- Many teachers and teams across the country have taken the work of James Beane and Barbara Brodhagen to heart and infused their classrooms with democratic principles and full student involvement in the curriculum development process.

- Mark Springer's *Soundings* explains in great detail how this Pennsylvania team has successfully brought alive the democratic approach to teaching and learning. The partner team leads students in selecting "affirmations" that become the classes' characteristics and goals, followed by formalizing guidelines as a Bill of Rights, and then living and learning all year in light of these beliefs.

- The Detroit Service Learning Academy has embedded service learning into their curriculum, K-8 (www.detroitservicelearning.org).

These teams and schools have high academic standards for their students. They help their students achieve the standards by going beyond discipline-specific information to spark a personal connection with students. The personal relevance of these connections inspires students to work hard for something more intrinsic and personally satisfying than just high grades. Students leave these classrooms better people, not just more informed students. Such stories are informative and inspirational to read, however, a team cannot merely adopt someone else's approach. They have to find ways to create unique adaptations that fit their situation. A team has to think deeply, just as these teacher-authors did, about what they value in the teaching and learning process and then formulate a way to implement those values. Implementation involves much more than posting the values or the "distinctions" on the wall. Teams need to not only define what they stand for but also figure out how they and the students can live and practice these values each and every day.

Here is a process that a team might use to begin the conversation that leads to action steps for the team:

1. Identify a block of time that is free from distractions and use it exclusively for serious thinking about team members' beliefs and goals.

2. Individually, have team members envision what their greatest hopes are for the team. It might be in narrative writing or visually presented in some way. Allow people to express themselves in the way most comfortable for them.

3. After everyone shares, the group identifies the common elements in each vision. Turn these common elements into "We believe" statements. For example: *We believe students should have an active role in determining the team's agenda,* or *We believe each of our students should have equal access to an intellectually stimulating curriculum,* or *We believe that interactive learning and appropriate scaffolding are key strategies to engaging and motivating our students and ensuring their ultimate success.*

4. Once the team identifies the "desired state," they plan specific steps in a timeline that will achieve that desired outcome. For example,

if a team wanted to fully integrate their curriculum using Project Based Learning (PBL) they might devise a plan with these steps:

Figure 1-1. Examples of team plan and timeline

Project Based Learning Plan

1. We decide what we need to know about PBL. (September)
2. We locate and study that information. (September)
3. Individual team members try one or two PBL units in their own disciplines. (October-November)
4. The team explores strategies for integrating across the curriculum. (December)
5. We design our problem-based unit. (January)
6. We implement, and evaluate a PBL integrated unit. (February)

Some energetic teams that are composed of "action first and fine-tuning as they fly" people may jump in with both feet and just go for doing an integrated unit immediately. A team has to have a good sense of self-awareness in order to decide which planning process or combination of them they will use.

5. The Internet provides opportunities for information gathering that have never existed before. Teams can search out via the Internet other teams that do the things their team would like to do and begin a digital conversation. One resource to consult is MiddleTalk Listserve www.nmsa.org/ProfessionalDevelopment/MiddleTalkListserv/tabid/1212/Default.aspx?PageContentID=198 (http://tinyurl.com/MiddleTalk)

6. The team also plans ways to determine how well they have been doing. What indicators should they be looking for? Will anecdotal evidence be available? Quantitative evidence? Will surveys be used? Time needs to be set aside regularly to self-assess and to maintain the vision as the focal point for their decision making and planning.

Next Steps

1 **Plan an integrated unit with the students being fully involved in determining what and how they will study.**
This may be a novel experience for students, but they will come to love it when their ideas, interests, and questions become the most important aspects of the unit. Some readers may start to shutter and shake at the idea of involving students in curriculum planning, as it is so alien, especially in this age of high stakes testing. Other readers, however, are pumping their arms in the air thinking, "Way to go!" But start small in a way that engages students big time while not making other teams or administrators nervous. For an idea of how to get started involving students in designing units, see Appendix A.

2 **Use advisory/homeroom time to provide students the opportunity to go beyond their immediate world and make life better for someone else via a service learning project.**
Nicholas Kristof in an article in *The New York Times* describes this type of work as "social entrepreneurship," and he profiled Talia Leman, who as a 10-year-old spearheaded a drive that raised $10,000,000 for victims of Hurricane Katrina. Young adolescents with their idealism and sense of fairness are primed to be social entrepreneurs. Share with them what others their age have done to make the world a better and more humane place. Here are several terrific resources for examples of young people making a difference:

- *The Teen Guide to Global Action: How to Connect With Others (Near & Far) to Create Social Change* by Barbara Lewis (2008, Free Spirit).

- RandomKid: The Power of ANYone www.randomkid.org

- Christopher Columbus Awards: Middle School www.christophercolumbusawards.com

Have students read some stories from these sources and then together analyze why students were able to accomplish these feats. Bring all of the advisory groups or homerooms together to share ideas for setting what Jim Collins in *Good to Great* calls a HAG, a Huge

Audacious Goal for the team centered on service to others. Work as a team to develop a plan of action. Lewis in *The Teen Guide to Global Action* suggests four steps to take in preparation for launching any action project (pp 7-18):

Figure 1-2.

How to Plan for an Action Project

1   Identify a cause. Some general categories include: human rights, hunger and the homeless, safety issues, environmental issues, and peace.

2. Research the cause. Research questions she suggests include among others:
    - "Where is the problem occurring?"
    - "Who is affected?"
    - "What are the short-and long-term effects of the problem?"
    - "What do the people in the affected areas want to happen?"

3. Plan your action
    - Volunteer
    - Organize
    - Advocate

4. Take action—Five steps from Lewis
    - Develop your mission.
    - Decide which specific actions you will take.
    - Create your timeline.
    - Brainstorm who might participate.
    - Plan your publicity.

Despite the fact that such a project may occur outside academic classes, students will be applying academic skills to this type of work— researching, reading, writing, speaking, presenting, using statistics, etc. But more importantly, engaging in such projects in which students are inspired to give of themselves in service helps them form a habit of mind that will follow them for a lifetime.

3 **Incorporate Real World Learning (RWL) approaches to units and lessons.** According to Michael Muir, Director of the Maine Center for Meaningful Engaged Learning (MCMEL), Real World Learning is coming to be a common term used to describe "... approaches that all contextualize high-value, standards-based content within the real world and the students' lives." RWL is meant to recognize that all these approaches have certain components in common (but in different combinations), rather than to debate the differences (or advantages) of each. The components of Real World Learning, according to Muir, are learning by doing, student voice and choice, higher order thinking, real world connections, and technology as a learning tool.

What does RWL look like? There is no one template. It may be a class that explores botany by studying and identifying the plants that grow along a town trail and then creates a display for the trail users to consult. Or it may be when a teacher recognizes that creating comics is a way to connect students with the curriculum. When students create digital stories using iMovie or share their work with the world via Voice Thread or communicate with experts from across the ocean, that's Real World Learning integrating technology as a learning tool.

What do these five RWL components look like in the classroom? Like most things in teaching and learning, there is no one perfect approach to any of these components. However, the chart in Appendix B provides specific classroom applications, many of which the reader will recognize. The last column of the chart lists suggestions for both print and Internet resources for implementing RWL into the classroom.

Teams can integrate the five RWL components into existing units. Try analyzing your next unit as in the example in Figure 1-3.

Figure 1-3.

Unit: *Roll of Thunder, Hear My Cry*

RWL Components	How This Component Is Integrated	Other Strategies I Might Integrate
Learning by Doing	Reader's Theater	
Student Voice and Choice	Choice in Final Project	Prereading work on understanding setting: generate student questions and integrate them into the unit.
Higher Order Thinking	Compare and contrast characters; evaluate character actions	
Real World Connection		Interview relatives who lived during the 1930s.
Technology		Create digital stories that tell family histories based on family interviews.

Real World Learning may sound like an exotic approach that requires totally revamping the curriculum. But in reality it means stepping back and looking at unit components with a critical eye. Look for ways to enrich the student learning experience by making content more relevant to the students' world and providing experiences that allow them to apply their learning. Incorporating technology, interactive learning strategies, and critical and creative thinking skills ensures that this process will engage students at many levels.

A note of caution: Unfortunately the "Green-eyed Monster" of jealousy often rears its ugly head when one or two teams in a school begin to think and act in innovative, creative ways. Other teams worry that they will be compared unfavorably, criticized, or pressured into doing things that push them out of their comfort zones. This phenomenon occurs in many schools. Julie Wood, a doctoral student at Harvard reported in 2000, "... although most teachers support student achievement, they are often ambivalent about, or even hostile toward, the success of their peers." It's not fun to be on the receiving end of colleagues' sarcasm and other verbal jabs. School leadership has a responsibility to work hard at building a collegial climate that values risk taking and sharing of academic success and challenges. Focusing on one or two teams who are doing things "right" is not helpful. All teams should be expected to regularly share successful approaches and strategies they are using. Individually and as teams, staff members need to gently remind the leadership team and one another that it is as important to have a safe and caring environment for staff as it is for students. The bottom line is that when the climate for staff is unhealthy and negative, those feelings trickle down to the students and impact their learning.

A last word from Jill...

Remember that making changes in one's pedagogy, as would be required when implementing any of the strategies described in this chapter, is never easy. It doesn't happen overnight or without support. But when it is apparent that the students' achievement and overall development will definitely benefit, teachers who are part of a fully functioning and mutually supportive team will readily make changes. There is an old adage or two worth mentioning:

- If we continue to do what we've always done, we will continue get the same results we always have.

- The only person's behavior we have control over is our own.

Individual teachers and teams have tremendous power to influence students' lives through their relationships, pedagogy, and vision of the possibilities education provides. Inspiring students to excel, become good people, and participate in the community in positive ways is a commendable and worthy professional and life mission.

2

Build Community and Foster 21st Century Skills

---

*The process of teaching students **how** to work together effectively is often skipped, and frustration results when group work becomes chaotic. Teams, however, can foster collaboration skills and build community in their classes so that collaborative academic work moves forward productively in a safe environment where everyone knows one another well.*

Learn by Doing

"We have to do what?" yelped Freddy as he stared wide-eyed at the red brick wall looming over his head.

Mr. Connors' voice boomed out over the asphalt parking lot. "Listen up! Your goal is to work as a group to place your piece of duct tape as high up on the wall as possible. And...you have to make sure everyone is safe." Tommy immediately grabbed his buddy Jason, and they began to trot toward the back door. "Guys, where are you headed? queried Mr. C.

"Gonna get a stepladder from the custodians," Tommy shouted back over his shoulder, still trotting at half speed.

"Whoa, back it up. No stepladders or any other equipment! Okay everyone gather round, let's go over the rules of this challenge.

- *Each advisory group's challenge is to place their tape as high up this wall as possible.*

- *You may not use any equipment.*

- *You have 15 minutes to problem solve this challenge. At 9:15 groups will stop what they are doing, and we'll check out where the pieces of tape are.*

Any questions?"

Each of the team's advisory groups huddled and began to spout off ideas. As the teachers meandered in and among the groups, they observed several things happening. In one group, students kept talking over one another, and in another the tallest member grabbed the tape and stood on his tiptoes and stuck the tape on the wall. The teachers had to bite their tongues and not intervene. They had agreed that this was to be a student-directed solution.

Groups began to try out their strategies. Ms. Nestor's group decided their tallest member would take a running start and then slap the tape on the wall as high as he could. The group cheered as he succeeded in getting it up to about six feet. Their cheers turned to moans when Mr. Toy's group was able to get their tape even higher by having the smallest boy stand on the shoulders of the tallest boy. Then both groups looked over at another group two cheerleaders were organizing. Using their experience with people pyramids, they helped half their group to build one that taped the highest point on the wall.

"OK, Let's gather and check out how well you did. I've got the tape measure—let's check. Wow! 7 feet 2 inches is the highest," said Mr. C.

Ms. Nestor then led a bit of processing. "Chat with a partner about what your group did to meet the challenge." After students shared their responses, she summarized the common ideas such as listening to everyone's ideas, settling on a strategy, and making sure that there were always people spotting climbers in any above-ground strategies.

"Back to your groups. You've heard what everyone did in order to be successful; now have a conversation about what you might do differently. You have another 15 minutes to strategize and find a way to get your tape higher than you did last time."

Immediately jumping to the challenge, the groups' energy was palpable. This time as the teachers watched and listened they observed that the groups were listening more carefully to one another, and they were incorporating strategies from other groups.

"Time," yelled Mr. Toy. The tape measure came out, and each group had bettered their own tape height on the wall. "Well done—everyone high five! OK, now find a partner, someone different from last time. Think about the processes you've just used in the last 45 minutes. How might these processes transfer to group work in our classes?" After mulling this question over, the students responded:

"We need to listen to each other."

"We need a plan!"

"We need to stop and look at our work and see how to make it better before we turn it in."

"Great ideas," said Mr. Toy. "Now we're going back in to advisory and do some individual reflection in our journals. Think about this question as we walk back to the team areas: 'What goal or desire does the tape represent in your life, and how might you use the lessons of today to achieve that goal or desire?'"

Mr. Connors had been taking notes of what the students had said during the processing, and he planned to make charts of the student ideas for reference during group work in their rooms.

———————————

This team of teachers believed that taking time to build community through physical challenges would help their students internalize skills they could use in the academic arena. They knew that it was critical to add the Reflect and Transfer piece to these challenges to help students make connections between the fun activities and the way they approached challenges in their own lives. The team had found a seemingly endless supply of ideas by Googling "team building activities" and planned to integrate many of these techniques into both advisory and classroom activities.

Build community and explicitly teach collaboration skills because:

- **Working collaboratively both in face-to-face and virtual situations in the digital world is a major component of models identifying 21st century skills.** The Partnership for 21st Century Skills (www.21stcenturyskills.org) framework includes interacting effectively with others and working effectively on diverse teams as one of its top skills. The enGauge 21st Century Skills (www.metiri. com/features.html) model includes effective communication: teaming, collaboration, and interpersonal skills. The International

Society for Technology in Education (ISTE) sets forth standards on communication and collaboration that include publishing with peers and contributing to a team to produce original works. People, of course, do not magically develop these skills; they need to understand what it means to be collaborative and to practice these desired skills. Middle grades teams are in a perfect position to advance these skills.

- **Middle school students learn best when they collaborate with others.** Studies show that "Students involved in cooperative work demonstrate higher levels of academic learning and retention than their peers working individually" (Frey, Fisher, and Everlove). Unfortunately, group projects are often less than successful because students have not been adequately schooled in working together. Frey and colleagues describe the participants in such work as the "worker bee, the gopher, and the hitchhiker" (p. 4). It makes sense for a team to work together to make sure that collaborative tasks are designed and implemented well and that students understand their responsibilities in the process. Common expectations, processing, and assessment practices used across the team will improve the quality of collaborative assignments.

- **Students also learn best in an environment that is psychologically as well as physically safe.** Strong, positive relationships that develop a sense of community in a group provide that sense of safety. "The school environment is inviting, safe, inclusive, and supportive of all" is one of National Middle School Association's 16 characteristics of effective schools for young adolescents. Teams are the major building block of the school environment, and team teachers cannot just sit back and hope a healthy team climate that supports collaboration will emerge like Athena bursting fully developed from Zeus's forehead. It is imperative that they actively craft activities, lessons, and experiences that build the desired environment and teach their students the skills to keep it alive.

- **Larger schools seem impersonal to the student.** Having a team identity helps students feel connected to a group that knows them and cares about them. Being a member of the Kennebec House or the Jupiter Team provides a personal connection that doesn't occur in schools without teams. Academic engagement, positive personal development, and group citizenship may all develop more effectively in schools where students feel attached, involved, committed, according to middle level experts Paul George and John Lounsbury (2000). Helping classmates solve challenges further solidifies this sense of belonging. Teams can challenge other teams to friendly competitions based on problem-solving challenges. Everyone benefits as a sense of community grows on the individual teams as well as across all teams.

Two Ways to Develop
the Team's Collaboration Skills

1 **Develop a set of team norms for yourselves.** Team teachers must develop respectful relationships with one another if they wish their students to exhibit such relationships in their group projects. Students notice how teachers interact, and any disrespect will be quickly noted. If the adults don't work as a team, chances are that the students won't either. One cannot model that which one doesn't practice regularly, so a first step calls for setting norms. This may be a fairly lengthy process, which, frankly, a school ought to use to set its staff norms. Unfortunately, a lot of people go through a norm-setting process only to watch them be ignored, thus making them skittish about taking the time to participate in the process again. Here's a short activity a team can use to set norms:

- Everyone writes down three behaviors he or she would appreciate from teammates during team meetings and one behavior that is simply a nonnegotiable for him or her. For example:
    - Focus on students' strengths rather than their weaknesses.
    - Don't correct papers while we're meeting.
    - Be on time (nonnegotiable).
    - Listen without interrupting.

- The nonnegotiables automatically become team norms (unless they are outrageous or unacceptable—then the team has to have some serious conversations).

- The team looks for commonalities among the other responses. These commonalities also become norms.

- The team discusses the behaviors only mentioned once and determines whether they are covered by the norms already identified. It's important to find out why the once-mentioned behaviors are important to the people who submitted them and then to negotiate an outcome everyone can abide. Although these conversations may be uncomfortable, it's time well spent in preventing a build-up of resentment that can later sabotage the team's relationships.

- Post the team norms and regularly reflect on how well the team is observing them. Don't just put them on the back shelf; effective teams gently hold each other accountable for following their agreed-upon norms.

2 **Identify the specific collaboration skills that students need.** Many of the skills required for success in group work are common speaking and listening skills in state standards such as: listening without interrupting; summarizing, paraphrasing, or adding to others' ideas; and asking questions to clarify someone else's idea. Other skills necessary for successful group work include planning a project from start to finish, locating resources, synthesizing information, and deciding on how to present the group's findings. This last set of skills is also categorized in most standards under research. After identifying all the necessary skills for group work, plan how the team will teach, reinforce, and assess these skills. Think also about how teachers will have students reflect on their individual and group progress as a precursor for assessing the work of the individuals and the group. This step is very important because individual and group accountability are key components in the process of successful group work (Frey et al.). Including interim steps of reflection and revision helps students improve the quality of their work before the final assessment, and results in less complaining and finger pointing about who did or did not do their share of the work.

Create daily reflection forms for everyone to use when involved in a collaborative effort. Teachers can use them as a Ticket Out the Door activity and review them to identify any groups that need an intervention or skills that need reinforcing. When students see similar expectations of individual and group accountability in all of their classes, they will realize that the teachers value this skill set. That which is valued is taken more seriously. Furthermore, by sharing with teammates how the students are doing with practicing their skills of collaboration, teachers provide valuable information for others as they plan future units involving group work.

Figure 2-1. *Self Reflection about collaboration*

Individual Reflection on My Group's Collaboration Efforts Today

1 = Really Need Improvemnet   5 = Totally Awesome

1. Today my group had a plan, and we stuck to it. Here is a list of what we accomplished:	① ② ③ ④ ⑤
2. Today my group listened to one another without interrupting.	① ② ③ ④ ⑤
3. Today, everyone in the group followed through on what they were supposed to do.	① ② ③ ④ ⑤
4. Today, I contributed to our group's project in a positive way, Here is how I contributed:	① ② ③ ④ ⑤
Tomorrow we need to:	

Next Steps

1 **Involve students in a year-long process of building collaboration skills.** Develop a mind-set about collaboration through group challenges that will build the desired collaborative culture. Hold team meetings that include student participation in decision making, and in academic classes build physical challenges that connect to the concepts under study. Such activities allow students to practice these skills in nonthreatening and fun ways. While some people shy away from the word "fun" when used in the context of school, they shouldn't. "Having fun is also a universal need. Fun is not necessarily synonymous with frivolity or silliness, though it sometimes can be both. It does mean engagement and fascination with what we do" (Kriete, 2002). Recent research studies show games and fun activities increase achievement. Use the novelty of physical challenges in an unexpected venue or incorporate humorous imagery into a serious discussion to entice students to engage in an activity that provides the needed practice of collaborative skills. Here are two suggestions to consider.

During the first week of school in a team meeting, use the following activity to nail down the team norms that will set the tone in every class. The process or skill students practice at each step of the activity is in italics in parentheses; this is an adaptation of Maine teacher Nancy Rideout's idea.

Figure 2-2. Activities build collaborative skills through practice.

Norm-Setting Activity

Find a space where all the students can gather comfortably and work in small groups. Have markers, chart paper, and a copy of the short book *The Class from the Black Lagoon* by Mike Thaler.

1. Break the team into groups of threes. *(Working with a variety of people.)*

2. Explain that the purpose of this meeting is for the students to establish how everyone will treat one another in every class. *(Being an active participant in a community decision-making process.)*

3. Read to the class with great vim and vigor *The Class from the Black Lagoon*, which is about a teacher who has been told that her class is just full of little rowdies.

4. Ask the small groups to reflect on the message they think the author wants to get across to his readers. A possible prompt might be "Talk in your groups about how expectations can affect the way we act or treat people."

5. Have groups share their ideas. *(Practicing a collaborative strategy that can be used in every class—Think, Pair, Share.)*

6. Challenge the groups to brainstorm as many characteristics of a horrible class from a "Black Lagoon" that they can think of. *(Working together to generate multiple solutions.)*

7. Have groups share. Chart their responses so everyone can see the list. *(Building in accountability by charting each group's responses.)*

8. Next, challenge the groups to brainstorm the characteristics of a "class from heaven." Have groups share and chart their responses. At this point the students have a lot to think about and use for the next steps.

9. Have groups reconvene and discuss what group behaviors are most important to ensure a class from heaven. Help students write the behaviors as positive statements instead of "don'ts". Ask each group to decide on the two behaviors they feel are most important. *(Learning how to reach consensus.)*

10. Chart each group's two behaviors. Because many will overlap, the easiest way to generate the list is to ask a group to share one, and then ask each succeeding group to share a behavior not already listed.

11. When the list is complete, ask each student to put a star on the behaviors most important to him or her. *(Holding everyone accountable for an opinion.)*

12. The number of stars will indicate which behaviors are most important to the group. They become the norms for the team and should be posted in each room and referred to regularly. The teacher may have additional expectations, but these are the norms for which students agree to hold one another accountable. *(Living with a group decision.)*

Most Important Behaviors

1. Be nice ★★★★★★★★★★★★★★★★★★★★★★★★★★★★★★★★★★★
2. Join in class discussions ★★★
3. Wait your turn to speak ★★★★★★★★★★★★★★★★★★
4. Respect other people's things ★★★★★★★★★★★★★★★★★★★★★
5. Do your fair share of the work ★★★★★★★★★★
6. Sharpen your pencil at the beginning of class ★
7. Help others how to use computer ★★★★★★★★★★★★★★★★
8. Be on time ★★★★★
9. Include everyone ★★★★★★★★★★★★★★★★★★★★★★★★★★★★★

This team might have six group norms: 1,3, 4, 5, 7, and 9.

- **Challenge activities.** Incorporate group challenges regularly. Not only do group challenges help develop a sense of community; but they also reinforce problem-solving skills, the ability to make and understand metaphors, innovative thinking, and the capacity to work in a collaborative manner. These are all skills that the next generation needs in order to thrive in a global economy. Teams make these activities purposeful by carefully crafting processing questions that require students to reflect, think metaphorically, and transfer learning to a different context.

There are a variety of resources, many of them online and providing descriptions and directions, for finding group challenges requiring few materials. One is at TeachMeTeamwork: http://tinyurl. com/teamwork123. Below are two challenges adapted from this website. The first, the Gordian Knot, offers processing questions designed to have students think metaphorically about the American Civil War. The second challenge, Bandana Relay, has been used to help students think about balancing equations. Metaphorical thinking is sophisticated, and students need lots of modeling and practice. Challenges are perfect vehicles for practicing this level of critical thinking because they are flexible enough to be used when the team is together as a whole or in individual classes.

Figure 2-3. Activity challenging students to think metaphorically

Gordian Knot With a Twist

Materials: Enough 24-inch lengths of rope to give one to each pair of students in the group. Use clothesline, 24-inch shoes laces, or comparable small rope.

1. Have students break into pairs. Give each pair a length of rope. Group the pairs into sets of 4 (8 people in a group). Each group of 8 forms a tight circle with pairs standing opposite one another grasping each end of their rope.

2. Keeping hold of the rope, members of the group should create a knot in the center of the circle by moving under and over one another while crisscrossing the circle. Be adamant that individuals not let go of the rope! Continue this knot tying process until there is only about 4 inches of rope remaining.

3. When the knots are complete, have each group carefully lower their knot to the floor. Each group then moves to another group's knot. Grasping the rope ends at the same time, the groups pick up the knots, and without letting go, untangle them.

4. Processing Questions:
   - What did your group need to do in order to succeed at this challenge? *(Reflection questions like this one reinforce the skills of collaboration.)*
   - In what ways is this activity like the life of an eighth grader at our school? Talk with a neighbor for a minute or two before we share as a group. Think about what the strings and the knot might represent. *(Starting with a question that relates the activity to the students' lives models the metaphorical thinking process in a concrete, nonthreatening fashion. Giving students an opportunity to talk with partners provides thinking and rehearsal time before having to speak in front of the entire group.)*
   - Now let's think about this activity and compare it to the unit we've been studying—the Civil War and Reconstruction Era. How are the making of the knot and then the untangling of it like the years 1850 to 1875? What might the string represent? What might the knot represent? Chat with your partner for a minute or two. *(The teacher should model with an example. "I think the string is like the abolitionists and the pro-slavery people who could only get themselves in a knot instead of resolving the issue of slavery.")*

In a personal communication April 16, 2009, Stephanie Kraft wrote about the next challange:

> *I tried out the bandana relay with my kids. I teach sixth grade math and was looking for students to make a connection between balancing the marble and balancing equations. Not only did they all thoroughly enjoy the activity, but many of them made the connection I was hoping they would, and once it was discussed, all students had that "Oh yeah, I get it" feeling! Then we continued to use it as a metaphor every time we talked about solving equations. We would say "Remember, you have to keep that marble from falling off," as in, "You have to balance your equation by doing the same thing to both sides." It was a very effective strategy.*

Figure 2-4. *Challenge activity for metaphorical thinking about balancing equations.*

Bandana Relay

Materials for bandana relay: bandana, paper or plastic cup, marble, or small ball

Teams must move from Point A to Point B.

- Split group into teams (4-8 people).
- Each person must hold onto the bandana with both hands.
- The bandana must be held out straight.
- The cup is balanced upside down on the bandana.
- The marble is perched on top of the cup.

- The team moves from Point A to Point B without dropping the marble; they must start over if the marble rolls off.

Processing questions:

- What strategies did your group use to solve this challenge?
- How might you adapt and apply these strategies in other situations?
- What do the marble, the cup, and the bandana each represent? What process that we have studied does this activity remind you of? Why?

Teams can use and reuse this type of challenge simply by changing some of the conditions or rules to make them more complex. Students have to adapt solutions that worked in the past, thus becoming more flexible thinkers. Ways to alter the conditions include using blindfolds for some members of the group, forbidding any oral communication, and "incapacitating" a hand or arm making mobility more difficult. Needless to say, safety always remains a primary condition.

- **Specific academic assignments.** In addition to challenge activities, students can build their capacities to work together while working on specific academic assignments. The building of discrete skills is a year-long process that begins with simple tasks of short duration and then moves gradually on to longer, more complex problems to solve.

Start small with Think-Pair-Shares that last for just a short time. Think, Pair, Share is a fantastic strategy because it takes just seconds to implement, taps into learning styles by giving internal processors time to think and external processors time to talk, and builds in summarization.

Figure 2-5. Short, simple tasks start skill building

Think, Pair, Share

1. After 10 or 15 minutes of instruction or reading, prompt the students to **think** about the lesson so far. Give them a specific prompt to focus their thinking. For example: What are 3 important characteristics of..., What is one of the important reasons..., or Write a one sentence summary of what we have discussed so far.
2. Have them **pair** up to **share** their thinking.
3. Have partners **share** their ideas with the class

There are many variations of this strategy. For example, students might role play a character from a book or a historical figure and think and share from that point of view, or one partner might summarize one topic while the other summarizes a related topic. (Partner A summarizes one perspective on an issue, and Partner B summarizes another. Partner A, pretend you are the moon, and Partner B you are the ocean lapping at the shores of coastal Maine. Explain to the other what you are doing/feeling as the tides rises and falls.) At Kaganonline.com one can purchase a Think-Pair-Share SmartCard which has 50+ ways to orchestrate this strategy.

If one team member teaches the students this strategy, then the other team teachers can easily integrate the strategy without having to take time to teach the process. They can have fun by inventing novel ways to implement it, and then share those ideas with their teammates. Common strategies used across the curriculum benefit everyone. Students develop confidence with the process and are willing to engage, and teachers save time by not having to teach a process every time they use a different strategy. Caution—don't overuse any one strategy!

Gradually introduce longer-lasting collaborative activities in which students learn how to sustain a working relationship with someone who is not their best buddy. Be transparent about what collaboration skills the students are working on, and begin to add in some self-reflection/assessments on the group work and the skills involved. Students recognize that teachers assess what they value, and valuing collaboration skills is a message worth sending. These longer sessions where student use collaborative skills in order to better understand content are setting the stage for full-fledged group work that is productive for each student. Again, there is the potential for teams to orchestrate together how and when these strategies are introduced and reinforced.

Two such strategies for deepening content understanding are Four Corners and Pictograph Summary. Team teachers, no doubt, have a number of other activities that fall in this category of short-time-span group work. Remember to model the desired collaborative behaviors when using any similar activity. Four Corners is another Spencer Kagan structure for cooperative or collaborative work. An adaptation of the Four Corners strategy is provided in Figure 2-6.

A Pictograph Summary asks students to summarize text or video or previous lessons using images that they create. The purpose of this strategy is for students to collaboratively synthesize information from one or more sources and then to recode this new learning in a different format (images). Recoding information (Sprenger, 2005) using non-linguistic representations, and cooperative learning (Marzano, 2001) are research-informed strategies that have a high probability of increasing achievement. Because everyone is not an artist, it's a good idea to model for students how line drawings, especially stick figures, can be very expressive depending on how arms, legs, and the head are positioned (Puentedura, 2010). Allowing students to practice before actually using these techniques in class is advisable. There are even websites that illustrate how to use stick figures. Check them out at http://tinyurl.com/stickfigures123 and http://tinyurl.com/stickfigures1234. The use of these websites and related ones would make a great agenda for a team meeting or advisory. Students could practice, place their best creations in a team gallery, and then use these skills in all of their classes. Here's the process that a team might use and adapt for its own purpose.

Figure 2-6. *Short, collaborative content activity*

Four Corners Activity
(adapted)

Ask students to move to a corner of the room whose label best matches their opinion, their knowledge level, their skill level, or represents something they like. What the corners are labeled depends on your purpose.

1. Each corner group is given a specific task, works together to accomplish it, and then presents to the entire group.

2. Here is a science example as it would play out in class:

    - Go to corner # 1 if you can clearly explain what a niche is.

    - Go to corner #2 if you can clearly explain what a habitat is.

    - Go to corner # 3 if you can clearly explain what an ecosystem is.

    - Go to corner # 4 if you can explain how a niche, habitat, and ecosystem are all related.

    - Corners 1, 2, and 3, your task is to create a chart that clearly explains your term. Use words and images.

    - Corner 4, your task is to create a graphic organizer that shows the similarities and differences among the terms and their relationship to one another (or to show this with images).

    - We will share our charts in 20 minutes.

Figure 2-7. Using images to summarize text or video

Pictograph Summary Activity

Decide what information will be the focus of the activity. It might be contained in something the students watch or read during the activity, or it could be information students have been studying for a couple of days.

1. Divide the students up into pairs or threes. Having more than three in the group runs the risk of one student not participating.

2. Give each group markers and a piece of chart paper. Working together, each group is to identify the four most important ideas to remember and to prioritize them. These points should be explained through images. At the bottom students list any questions or ideas they still do not understand.

3. Remind students the skills of collaboration they should be practicing—listening without interrupting, restating what someone else has said, or generating several ideas before settling on the best one.

4. Reinforce the point that they will be held individually accountable. The teacher can decide whether these assessments are formal or informal in nature.

Pictograph Summary	
Point #1	Point #3
Point #2	Point #4
Questions we still have:	

5. Because the information from all groups will be similar, it might not be worth the time to have each group report out. Instead, pair groups up and have them share their ideas. Then give groups time to review their Pictograph Summaries to see if they are still satisfied with the ideas they have identified. It's important to establish the pattern of revising work to improve its quality, which is a habit that the all the students on the team need to develop and use in every class.

Design extended group work to build on the lessons learned though Think-Pair-Shares and short-time-span group work and to incorporate the elements proven to make group work productive. Frey, Fisher and Everlove (2009) have synthesized the information on why group work often goes awry in classrooms and what needs to be in place to ensure high quality work. They identify six essential elements to embed within the instructional plan:

- Using positive interdependence: Interdependence includes common goals, shared resources, and assigned roles.

- Promoting face-to-face interaction: Groups should not simply divide up the work and go their separate ways. They need to be continually sharing information, clarifying ideas, and deciding on next steps.

- Ensuring individual and group accountability. When group work is less than productive, leaving out individual accountability is often a factor. Both the individual student and the group as a whole need to receive descriptive feedback on a regular basis.

- Building interpersonal and small group skills: Important 21st century skills need to be modeled and practiced as part of the group work process.

- Incorporating group processing: Leaving out the step of group reflection and process is another step often overlooked in the past. Students cannot transfer skills to a new context unless they have time to evaluate what worked and what didn't.

- Providing a meaningful task: Middle school philosophy has included challenging and relevant curriculum as critically important for over 30 years. Group work tasks need to fit that descriptor (pp. 15-20).

All of these elements have been part of cooperative learning models for more than two decades. Unfortunately, in the past some steps were rushed through or ignored with the resulting frustration of students and teacher leading to the abandonment of this powerful learning experience. Team members should support one another as acting in the role of a critical friend to give feedback on developing projects. *"Wow, Kendall, this project is really going to appeal to the students because you are using managing a hip hop group as the jumping off point. I'm wondering, however, where you have built in time or an approach for group processing?"* Kendall receives descriptive feedback from her teammate and has information to reshape the unit so it will be even more successful. Helping one another fine tune instructional plans is an opportunity teams should not overlook!

3 **Think digital collaboration. In this day and age collaboration between individuals and groups often happens virtually half a world away.** Schools are remiss if they do not look for ways to revise their curriculums to include this new reality. Participants in Web seminars using Adobe Connect (adobe.com/ap/products/connect) or Elluminate (www.elluminate.com) are listening, viewing, and processing a presentation while monitoring a chat box where they might choose to make a comment, ask a question, or respond to another participant's comment. During the Web seminar, they also have opportunities to raise their digital hands and speak directly to all the other participants. What a different experience than working with a group face-to-face! This kind of "meeting" is only going to become more common, and people who are adept and comfortable with using this technology are at an advantage. It is head-in-the-sand behavior for schools not to teach students this new form of communication (both the technology and behavioral skills that apply). Many schools are using virtual learning environments like Moodle (www.moodle.org) and StudyWiz (www.studywiz.com) to create environments where this type of collaboration can exist. Mark Hatch, principal of Messalonskee Middle School in Oakland, Maine, shared in a webcast that Moodle has allowed his students to share ideas across classes, teams, and grade levels.

Todd Williamson, a science teacher from New Bern, North Carolina, has been experimenting with Chatz (www.chatzy.com), a Web tool that allows for private chats to occur. He uses it with his science classes as a "backchannel" opportunity for conversation about a video the students are viewing. Backchannel is defined in *Wikipedia* as "the practice of using networked computers to maintain a real-time online conversation alongside live spoken remarks." He reports mixed results but is still enthusiastic about the possibilities (Personal communication, January 18, 2010). The first time he experimented with this tool the students were viewing a less-than-exciting video on the research process. To keep students focused, he set up a Chatz chat and posted questions and links related to the video for the students to respond to as they watched. Students remained engaged in the lesson despite the dry presentation of the material and learned most of the major ideas presented. Another experiment using Chatz in conjunction with a fast-paced science video had less positive results because of the video's dense content material. In this case the students really needed to give their full concentration to just the one source. A lesson learned was that, as with any strategy, one has to consider the purpose of the instructional plan and choose the approaches most appropriate for the goals and materials used in the lesson. Backchanneling and virtual learning environments are just two ways to teach students how to collaborate in their digital world.

Opportunities for global collaboration among students are growing. ePals (www.epals.com) is an example of a website that teams can tap into as they develop exciting and intellectually stimulating learning experiences for their students. Because this type of collaboration is only going to expand, team teachers along with their students need to experiment in a safe way with these opportunities. Also, at the rate that Web tools are being invented, it is necessary for teams to reevaluate regularly how they are teaching their students global digital collaboration skills.

A last word from Jill...

We all need to remember that the life skills students need to master through activities such as the ones presented in this chapter are as important as the content itself. And they are at the same time highly effective in helping students understand that content. Collaboration and problem solving have simply become universal skills for anyone wanting to achieve success in today's world. Schools have to take the lead in developing them in their students, and collaborative teaching teams are the frontline role models for the next generation.

3

Make the Most of Common Planning Time

Common planning time is often swallowed up discussing the same few students, filling out reports that don't lead to a change in behaviors, or just talking with other staff members who stop by. Substantive conversations on team goals, curriculum, and instruction never seem to occur. Teams have to become collaborative problem solvers to protect this valuable time for its prime purpose.

Team Meeting

Team Leader: Ok—here's what we need to do before Mrs. Smith arrives.

Team member #1: Mrs. Smith again? This must be her 3rd or 4th visit this year—and nothing ever changes!

Team leader: Well, we need to keep trying. Here are the special ed kids' progress reports—let's see if we can get them filled out before the conference. Tomorrow the counselor wants to talk about Sally who is failing 3 out of 4 of our classes.

Team member #2: Here we go again!

Team member #3: WAIT! STOP! Let's not do this anymore. Wasn't it Einstein who defined insanity as doing the same thing over and over and expecting a different outcome? We've been filling out reports and having multiple parent conferences with no visible results, and whatever plan we come up with lasts for about a day-and-a half.

Team member #2: So...should we just ignore poor performance and bad behavior?

Team member #1: We're helpless...we don't get any support from home.

Team member #3: Look, I'm frustrated too, but I'm not suggesting we give up. Rather, I'm suggesting we rethink our process and do some problem solving.

Team member #1: We're working as hard as we can. We can't take on more.

Team member #3: I'm thinking "different" not more.

Team member #2: What do you mean by different?

Team member #3: Well—I think we first have to identify what the issues really are, and why our approaches might not be working..... and then go looking for some fresh ideas. For example, I think one issue is that we lose track of kids and how they're doing academically and socially. Then we have a crisis, and we have to scurry around looking for a solution. Surely there is a system we can use among ourselves to keep better track of our kids.

Team leader: I think another issue is that we have students who weren't successful last year and probably weren't in elementary school. We don't know what strategies were ever used with these students. Maybe we should find out if any successes were recorded.

Team member #1: Hmmmmmmmmmm. I'm not convinced anything we do will make a difference.

Team member #2: Well, I'm not sure either, but I agree it is insanity to keep doing the same thing over and over and not make progress. Let's start small. (Looking at team member #3) I bet you have some ideas from those graduate classes you've been taking. Let's hear one!"

Team member #3: (Big grin) Did you know that most folks just expect students' motivation to decrease when they hit middle school? But there are at least three patterns that impact student motivation...

This team seems to be at a crossroads. Will they continue to do what they've always done, getting the same results, or will they step out of their comfort zones and look for new solutions, perhaps ones suggested by recent research? Highly functioning, proactive teams need time together to do complex problem solving, which makes common planning time a particularly valuable commodity. Teams, therefore, must dedicate this time to the work they have identified as critical to helping students develop their academic and personal potential.

Common planning time is an essential component of teaming if the desired benefits of teaming are to be realized. Necessary conversations that directly impact student learning need to be held daily if the team is to be nimble in addressing student learning and social-emotional needs as well as in planning strategically to meet standards that cut across the curriculum. Bi-monthly or once-a-week team meetings after school cannot possibly afford teams the necessary time to be effective or innovative. *Applying Middle Grades Research to Improve Classrooms and Schools* (Flowers, Mertens, Mulhull, and Krawczyk, 2007) is an excellent source of supporting research on the power of common planning time. Multiple studies found that teams were more successful in meeting student needs and delivering curriculum when they met almost daily. The result was increased student achievement and happier and more confident students.

One critical aspect of collaborative teamwork is addressing student behavior. Disruptive or disengaged students take away positive learning time from both themselves and other students. Middle grades team teachers with common planning time have the advantage of being able to work in concert to help these students redefine their academic lives. Studies such as *The Forgotten Middle* (ACT, 2008) and *Putting Middle Grades Students on the Graduation Path: A Policy and Practice Brief* (Balfanz, 2009) clearly show how important the middle grades are to students' futures. Middle grades teams cannot settle for "good enough." They must strive to motivate each and every student to work at his or her highest potential while recognizing that one approach is insufficient to meeting this goal. And it is in common planning time when plans are made to make this happen.

Ways to Increase a Team's Effectiveness

- **Designate which common planning periods will be committed to teamwork and which to parent conferences or other special purposes**. Barring real emergencies, hold to these decisions. Simply do not schedule meetings, complete paperwork, or be available to anyone wandering by your meeting room. Consider putting a very polite "Team at Work! Please Do Not Disturb" sign on the door that invites people to leave a message or e-mail you. Although this may sound like a cold, unsociable practice, teams must have uninterrupted time to focus on the academic, social, and emotional lives of all of their students. Talk about your intention to put up such a sign with the building administration. The principal undoubtedly understands this problem and may well make it a matter for discussion by the entire faculty.

- **Work toward consistency across the team in classroom management practices.** Identify which classroom management strategies or techniques each member of the team can commit to, and then hold each other accountable by doing check-ins every so often. Though teachers often consider classroom management style a personal matter, consistency across the team on major management issues sends a definite message to students about expectations in all team classrooms and eliminates the whining as students attempt to play one teacher off another. A consistent and effective approach to behavior issues is an important element in achieving that desired positive team climate. Because the reality of the classroom sometimes builds up enough steam to cause gaskets to blow and good intentions to fly out the window, taking time to debrief volatile issues is a good use of team time—everyone learns something by talking about what happened and discussing alternative ways of reacting. It's also a sign that a team has developed healthy relationships when members feel free to discuss difficult situations.

- **Bond with special education colleagues and others who work with a particular group of students, such as English language learners and gifted and talented students.** Perhaps you can create opportunities to team teach with these specialists. When teaching in the same classroom, teachers invariably learn from one another. For example, the classroom teacher may not realize that some of her students thrive on predictability and consistency in practices such as posting of assignments, collecting papers, and seating arrangements. After team teaching with the special ed teacher who offers that observation, the classroom teacher can tweak her practices to increase the comfort level of those particular students and remove a barrier to learning. The special educator, on the other hand, may never have used student questions as a basis of an instructional plan. By observing how student-generated questions motivate both special ed and regular ed students, he may adapt that strategy in his self-contained classes. Inevitably, all the students benefit from having more than one teacher in the room, and teachers can work together proactively to head off learning and behavior issues.

- **Use the research on motivation to develop fresh and thoughtful approaches to helping recalcitrant or disengaged students get back on track, or perhaps even find that track for the first time.** Anderman and Midgley wrote an *Eric Digest* article entitled "Motivation and Middle School Students" in which they report some useful findings:

  - The commonly accepted belief that a decline in motivation as students enter middle school is to be expected is not necessarily valid.

  - Students' beliefs about why they are or are not successful are a powerful motivator. This is called Attribution Theory.

    - Students with a history of failure are less likely to be motivated to engage in learning activities.

    - If students think that the power to succeed is determined by things beyond their control, then they often lack motivation.

    - If students believe their lack of success is determined by their poor study habits, then they are more likely to eventually try to succeed (A student's personal belief is not the same thing as hearing a teacher point out this connection.)

  - When setting goals with students, it is more effective to focus on a task rather than an acquisition of knowledge. This pattern is referred to as Goal Theory.

  - Meeting three sets of needs in the young adolescent—"sense of competence, relatedness to others and autonomy"

(Anderman and Midgley)– is another strong motivational force. This last approach is called Self-Determination.

Van Hoose, Strahan, and L'Esperance (2001), report that studies repeatedly show that students who are motivated to learn feel "valued, able, and responsible." They go on to report on a highly successful school-designed program that successfully addressed the neediest of their students. "The staff there believed that the barriers to academic success were embedded primarily in social and emotional concerns, and once those barriers are removed, students can focus more fully on academics" (p. 62).

Recognizing these conditions that relate to motivation, a team could eschew the currently popular approaches to solving behavior and motivation issues and formulate fresh approaches. Here are several ideas to consider and discuss during common planning time:

- Identify the repeat offenders. Consider behavioral miscreants, students who are failing due to missing work, and those who slouch in the back of the room refusing to engage in learning activities.

    - Be detectives and find out if this is new behavior or long-standing.

    - Have informal conversations to tease out students' thinking. They won't admit to an adult that they are not working because they feel incompetent. However, key phrases like "the work is stupid" or "I'm never going to use this" may be indicators that the student feels stupid. Also try to find out whether they believe others succeed just because they're smart. Such insights can help the team discover ways to build students' confidence in academic abilities and help them understand that they do have control over their degree of success.

    - Negotiate. Find a way to get the child to begin work or focus more seriously. A conversation might go something like this...*We notice you don't like to write, and we bet you don't like receiving the low grades on your writing either. We want you to succeed and worry that low grades keep you from really trying. So how about this? We won't put a letter grade on your essays. We'll make comments and suggestions and just put a check in the grade book. It will not hurt your grade. When you are ready to start putting a grade on your writing assignments, we will.* (Author aside: I used this strategy successfully with students. Within one or two assignments the students gave me the go-ahead to start grading. They just needed to stop equating a grade with self-worth.)

– Set a task goal with students and build in feedback *before the assignment is due* that explicitly explains what next steps to take to improve the quality of work.

– Celebrate small steps forward by specifically recognizing the behavior responsible for the success.

– Do not fall for the argument "This is not fair to the rest of the kids." What's not fair to the students is another student acting out and consuming valuable learning or teacher-interaction time.

- Make sure every child on the team has an adult advocate. Dropouts always report that not feeling connected is one of the reasons they did not stay in school. A long time ago Jean Mizer wrote a short story entitled "Cipher in the Snow" that was later the basis for an NEA film widely used in the 50s and 60s. It's the story of a teenager, an isolate at school, who dies in a snow bank. When a teacher tries to organize a group from his school to attend the funeral, he can't even find ten people who knew the student well. We would all like to believe that this couldn't happen at our school. To find out if that is the case, try this test during a common planning time. Spread out individual pictures of your students on a table. Have each teacher on the team put a star on the picture of each student about whom he or she can share two nonacademic facts. Step back and look at the array. How many student faces have no stars or only one? Typically, quite a few. This little exercise points out the need for teams to actively ensure that each of their students is connected to an adult who knows them, talks with them, and thereby builds a relationship.

- Keep boredom at bay by building in more choice and challenge for students. Choice is a simple way to provide students with autonomy, giving them decision-making power in their own learning process and helping to fight boredom. Boredom is a major contributor to student lack of effort. As Ben Johnson relates in his *Educatopia* blog,

> *Recently, I asked a 14-year-old student why he was struggling in school. He explained that it's because school is boring. To be blunt here, when I recently took five days and followed one student each in first grade, third grade, sixth grade, eighth grade, and ninth grade all day long through each of their classes, I was bored most of the time. I found it hard to sit still for so long, and I wondered how the students got through it.*

In *Philanthropy News Digest*, a posting, "Most Dropouts Leave School Due to Boredom, Lack of Encouragement, Report Finds," summarizes the findings of a Gates Foundation study. Boredom was the major reason 50 percent of the study's subjects said they dropped out of school (2006). Some would argue that students are bored because they just do not want to work hard. However, studies do not back up that assertion. Study after study (investigating the consequences of detracking on student achievement [Burris, Wiley, Welner, and Murphy, 2008], increasing academic "press" in the middle grades [Mertens and Anfara, 2006], tracking students' understanding and retention of science concepts through "hard fun" [Berry and Wintle, 2009]) shows students react positively to challenging curriculum delivered in a developmentally appropriate manner. Choice and challenge are two deterrents to boredom and student lethargy.

- Give students the feedback they need to improve their work before the final due date, and be clear that acting on this information will increase their chances for success. Such feedback is a critical component of building students' sense of autonomy and feeling of competence. Moreover, the type of feedback is extremely important to their learning. A "well done" or "good job" does not adequately build students' understanding of what specific aspect of the work is "good," and they often cannot then transfer that same device or strategy to other work. Also valuable is timing the feedback that explains the next steps students must take to improve their work to come before the final assessment is made. Research indicates that just giving feedback increases student learning more than giving grades or even giving grades plus feedback (Wiliam, 2006). Grades did not help the learning process in this study.

These ideas can be off-putting because they may require team members to change long-held teaching practices and beliefs, not an easy feat. One of the advantages of being on a team is that there is a built-in support system. One can dialogue with teammates, feel free to say, "I just don't get this," ask for feedback, and problem solve—all within a nonthreatening and nonjudgmental atmosphere. Overheard at a middle level conference was this interesting and pertinent statement, "Teaming equals professional development each and every day." The opportunity to continuously learn from one another is, indeed, a form of professional development that results in more effective practices in the classroom.

Consider Using Common Planning Time to...

1 Institute a "Kindness Crew" with the goal of being the kindest middle grades team in your state where everyone fits in and no one feels isolated. "Impossible!" you say? Maine's Biddeford Middle School set out to become the kindest middle school in the state and in the process has had a positive effect on both the school and wider community. A team could use a similar approach to create a team climate of kindness and mutual respect. In Biddeford a small group of teachers began the work with Michael Chase of the Kindness Center (www.thekindnesscenter.com/the_kindness_center/

home.html). Although having a partner in this type of venture is a real plus, it is not a necessity. Here are some of the major components of the Biddeford program that a team could adapt for its own situation (Chase, Mullins, and Sferes, 2009).

- Develop a set of core values the initiative will revolve around. The Biddeford group used the Kindness Center's 9 Elements of a Kind Heart: attentive, authentic, charitable, compassionate, courageous, enthusiastic, grateful, inspirational, and patient. It never works well just to adopt another group's values; they need come from within each group.

- Recruit students to be part of the planning and implementing of the initiative—the Kindness Crew. Make sure their work is authentic.

- Find ways to incorporate the values throughout the work of the team. In Biddeford the teacher planners, using ideas from the students, developed a series of lesson plans for use in advisory period.

- Help everyone—students and staff—live the core values. The Biddeford group shared specific ways teachers could exemplify the values. For example, teachers were encouraged to be attentive by stopping what they were doing when the students entered their room and by really listening to them. Other suggestions related to being in tune with the changes in nature and the environment and to being more attentive to colleagues in meetings and the staff room. For students they developed a rubric that gave examples of applying the 9 elements at school, in the community, at home, and in nature.

- Value the efforts by making the work visible. Students made paper chains—each link represented an act of kindness. The chains were made in homeroom and linked together for the final assembly. The end result was an awesome display of 3200 acts of kindness that stretched for 200 feet.

- Include a community outreach project. Every community has opportunities for students to get involved.

Check out the Biddeford Middle School Kindness Crew at
http://bmskc.edublogs.org

Figure 3-1. Composed of 3,200 links and 200 feet long, the Kindness Chain
at Biddeford Middle School took 60 students to carry it.

2 **Find ways to provide students with authentic audiences for the sharing of their work.** On January 30, 2010, participants in a workshop at Educon 2.2 in Philadelphia created a book in one session that was shared on the web via SlideShare.net. In two hours there were over 600 hits; in two weeks, over 4000. The book is called *Field Guide for Change Agents* and can be viewed at http://tinyurl.com/slidebook123. Imagine what a team could do with this one Web 2.0 tool to build students' confidence and pride in their work.

- Students could "create" a book that showcases their work in an integrative unit.

- Individual students could share with parents and grandparents math processes they have mastered by using digital cameras, white boards, or SmartBoards.

- Classes could share the conclusions from a science experiment they designed and receive feedback from interested people across the globe.

For years, teachers have documented the power of an authentic audience to inspire students to energetically and thoughtfully tackle a project. Here are excerpts from an article by Steven Levy in *Ed Leadership*:

> Laura had been particularly excited about learning expeditions…
>
> During the first three weeks of school, however, she received different feedback from her students—numerous eye rolls and incessant grumblings. All the activities she thought would appeal to them were greeted with yawns."
>
> The next week I visited Laura's class, told some stories about the conflict in Guatemala, and showed some photographs from San Juan Cotzal. Laura introduced the idea of making books to send to the children. In a short time, Spanish class was transformed from 'Gotta do boring worksheets' to 'Can we make books to send to these kids in Guatemala?

Team teachers can teach one another or learn from their students how to use VoiceThread, Animoto, Glogster, SlideShare, Xtranormal and all of the various safe sites for students to publish their writing. Publishing for the world is much different than publishing just for the teacher. Twelve-year olds may be ambivalent about whether the teacher appreciates their work or thinks they are smart. However, those same twelve-year olds do not want to appear like "dorks" in front of their digital peers whether they be in a partner school across an ocean or on a social-networking site that posts creative writing, opinions, or reviews. Posting student work on the web that may be commented on is a motivator for middle grades students to take the extra time to improve the quality of their work. Pride in one's work becomes a habit, and positive feedback from an authentic audience builds confidence. Using digital tools also provides teachers an opportunity to discuss digital citizenship and the concept of digital footprints and how one's digital tracks will follow him all his days.

Providing an authentic audience does not have to be a high tech activity. Invite everyone you can think of to attend class when students are presenting. Grab the principal, the counselor, the secretary, the class next door, or the custodian for a half hour. Invite senior citizens to join the class. It's often difficult to pull in folks during the day;

however, there are some stay-at-home parents and other community members who would be honored to be included and willing to give feedback to students.

Of course the best way to provide an authentic audience is when the students are involved in a project that serves a real purpose similar to the Spanish students writing books for children in Guatemala or presenting the results of their research on safe playgrounds before the city council. Sometimes it's daunting to plan and implement units that are not based on a textbook, however, a team with its multiple experiences and talents can tackle obstacles together. Common planning time provides a team of teachers with the opportunity to craft these effective and rigorous learning opportunities together.

3 **Prepare for morning or team meetings.** Educators have used class meetings for a variety of purposes for years. Some approaches such as the Responsive Classroom® have formalized the concept into an integral part of their program. It's always interesting to review the thinking of such groups as a way to inform one's own practice. For example, the Responsive Classroom® program gives several reasons for beginning the day with a morning meeting: a morning meeting sets the tone for the day, attends to the social and emotional needs of students for belonging and feeling valued, and merges social, emotional, and academic learning.

Other models use class meetings as a way to solve problems and plan events, or in some cases, middle grades educators use a class meeting approach to actually plan curriculum with students. Gert Nesin and Todd McKinley from the Leonard Middle School in Old Town, Maine, hold a morning meeting each day when the students return from Allied Arts. The meeting may last from 5 minutes to 30 minutes. Because Nesin and McKinley are a two-person team, they can easily adjust the schedule. They use the morning meeting for a variety of purposes. It's one way the entire team reconnects with one another, especially after the weekend or vacation. It is a time for recognition and announcements. It also is a time when any potentially difficult situation can be addressed before it becomes a crisis. Finally, morning meeting is a time to review and set up the learning plans for the day. Morning meeting has allowed this team to develop healthy relationships and a sense of belonging between and among teachers and students (G. Nesin, personal communication, January 21, 2010).

 Share ideas for incorporating age-appropriate strategies across the curriculum using three simple principles:

- **Keep the work engaging.** Michael Yell, a social studies teacher from Wisconsin, is quoted in *Managing the Madness* as saying, " I have not said or done anything regarding rules in my 7th grade classes for years. Far more important, I believe, is that from day one you engage your students in their learning" (p. 92). Monte Selby in a MiddleTalk posting shared these wise words from John Lounsbury, middle level philosopher and sage: "'Do you know what you should be teaching in your class tomorrow?' Then he answered, 'It doesn't matter. Tomorrow, just get them fully engaged in something—so engaged they want to get messy and up to their ears in it.' He went on, 'Once you have them fully engaged, do you know what you should teach the next day? It doesn't matter. Just get them fully engaged in something'" (Selby, 2009).

  The reader may be drumming his or her fingers right now and thinking, "I work very hard but the students just don't respond because…" Mike Muir, who has devoted much of his career to trying to understand underachievers and how to make schools work for all students, urges us not to play the fruitless blame game. Instead, he has developed a Meaningful Learning model that encapsulates elements of learning that engage students. This model highlights student voice and choice, real world connections, learning by doing, an inviting school, and higher order thinking. In addition, teachers who integrate Web 2.0 and other digital tools into their lesson plans beyond simply manufacturing digital worksheets find their students more engaged in class work. By engaging students at full speed, team members will circumvent behavior and disengagement issues that bog down common planning time and leech away valuable time that should be spent collaboratively strategizing developmentally responsive ways to address the cognitive, social, psychological, and physical needs of their students.

⚡ • **If students have been "sitting and getting" for 10 minutes, insert an opportunity for an interactive episode.** If teachers don't provide regular opportunities for movement and interaction, students will find inappropriate ways to squirm, stretch, and chat. It just makes more sense for the teacher to orchestrate active time for students to review information, brainstorm solutions, or share ideas rather than wasting time disciplining. If teammates use similar structures for these interactions, then students become very adept at implementing them without having to hear the directions repeated every time—a time-saving team strategy. Furthermore, research does suggest that summarization and continuous use of review strategies increases student understanding (Sprenger, 2009). Here are three great resources for finding these types of activities:

> – *Everyone's Invited! Interactive Strategies That Engage Young Adolescents* published by NMSA: http://tinyurl.com/jillspencer
>
> – Kagan Online Magazine: www.kaganonline.com/Newsletter/index.html
>
> – Active Learning Strategies: http://tinyurl.com/activelearning123

Resources

• **Use multiple ways to demonstrate learning, even for class assignments and homework.** There are loads of reasons why a one-size-fits-all approach is ineffectual and not worth falling on one's sword for. Fine-motor skill development, processing styles, time needed for processing information, and cognitive development are all in flux in the middle grades. A team that helps one another figure out alternative ways for students to "pass in" assignments that still demonstrate progress and understanding will be creating a team climate that invites students to participate in a positive manner.

Here are some ideas to adapt and use, especially if the assignment is not designed to assess writing skills:

- Math classwork/homework: some students seem to work better in a large space rather than on a piece of paper. Consider having students with this need do their work on a white board and snap a digital picture to document their effort and knowledge.

- Allow auditory learners to make mp3 files or use computer speech capabilities to record their responses to assigned questions or to do their planning for a writing task.

- Encourage the visual learners to identify important ideas in text or produce visual evidence of new learning by drawing cartoons using Web 2.0 tools such as Animoto and Glogster or by creating original two-or three-dimensional non-linguistic representations. Here is an example of a pictorial explanation of the Pythagorean Theorem.

Figure 3-2. Using wall tiles to demonstrate understanding of the Pythagorean Theorem (Fossum Middle School, McAllen Texas).

A last word from Jill...

"All of us are smarter than any one of us" is a silly little saying that holds great truth like the old adage, "Two heads are better than one." Common planning time is too valuable for teachers to spend day after day filling in reports and revising discipline plans that rarely get results. Thinking together, a team can develop innovative strategies that are research-informed and thereby more likely to change student behaviors that erode the enthusiasm and energy of everyone involved. However, teacher behavior also has to change. For a team to acknowledge that long-held practices are ineffective and then step away from them takes courage, and it takes collaboration. The payback, of course, is that more of the team's students will be happier, achieve at higher levels, and be better prepared for what lies ahead.

We all need to remember that kids, especially young adolescents, develop at different rates in a variety of physical, physiological, and social ways. Although middle schoolers are at a vulnerable time in their lives, we must find ways to build the skills and the confidence they will need in their future schooling and beyond. What works for 15 students isn't going to work for 10 others. Fair is when all students are held to the same high standards, but have access to different ways to meet them. When by our collaborative teamwork we can decrease the unsociable and disruptive actions of our students, our instructional time will be more pleasant, less stressful, and more productive. In these days of budget cuts, it is imperative that we use the hard-fought-for common planning time fully and professionally, so boards of education will resist the temptation to eliminate this key component of the middle school.

4

Help Students Develop Key Organization Skills

Too many folks think a 13-year old should be able to organize his or her life effectively even though recent brain research suggests that organization skills aren't fully developed until the late teens or early 20s. A team, however, can scaffold these skills for students so they have a better chance for success.

Organizational Dilemmas

Mariah's long, wavy hair flashed as she whirled around in her seat. First diving into her book bag, then madly flipping through her notebook, she was quickly destroying her little piece of the classroom. Her frustration was obvious as she kept returning to search her backpack and then clawing through the various notebooks on her desk. "I did my homework!" she gasped. "It's here somewhere." Mariah was an excellent student and not used to being unprepared.

Her teacher, a bit perturbed by the disturbance Mariah's actions were causing in the classroom, replied, "Calm down, you'll find it. Let's just go on."

Mariah whipped around and snapped out, "Why aren't you doing your job? You're supposed to keep us organized!"

Three thousand miles across the country, another young adolescent, clearly overtired and stressed by juggling school work, soccer, music lessons, and multiple other activities, complained petulantly to his mom, "Why did you let me get involved in everything!?! You're supposed to protect me from myself."

And, elsewhere a student-parent-teacher conference is in progress to explore remedies for continuously late work. The mother looks first at her son and then at the teacher, "He is 13 years old; it's time for him to manage his own homework."

Whose job is it—students', teachers', or parents'—to ensure middle grades students are organized, prepared for class, and able to handle varied responsibilities? Answer—everyone's, because young adolescents need all the help they can get in developing organizational skills that will serve them in school as well as later in life.

Students' organizational ability is important because:

The ability to (1) organize and keep track of materials, (2) plan and organize one's time, (3) study and master new materials independently, and (4) discern which resources will be the most useful are all skills necessary in school, the workplace, and in one's personal life. These are critical life skills needed to become a flexible thinker and lifelong learner able to respond to future challenges. These skills have always been important, but have become critical in a global society. The Partnership for 21st Century Skills (www.21stcenturyskills.org) calls for self-direction skills and *enGauge 21st Century Skills* (www.metiri.com/features.html) calls for high productivity skills.

These skills, of course, do not develop on their own; patterns need to be established, and strategies must be learned and practiced through modeling and guided activities. We also need to help parents figure out how they can contribute to helping their children develop these skills. Parents might find help on the parent-created website http://momshomeroom.msn.com, which is full of tips for supporting children with homework and projects. Share it with parents at a curriculum night or in a newsletter. Be sure to explain how the topics on the website directly connect with the work students do in your classes.

Expectations for students in the middle grades grow astronomically from those they had in elementary school—multiple teachers, assignments, rules, and opportunities for engaging in co-curricular activities, not to mention multiple new friends, all of which need to be juggled, sorted, and figured out by our 10- to 15-year olds. All of these "multiples" affect their work habits, attention spans, and concentration. Mastering organizational skills presents a huge learning curve for middle grades students, but such skills are an integral part of student achievement and success.

The front cortex of the brain is the site of the ability to develop a plan of action and carry it out, work through the steps of problem solving, ferret out important information, and control one's impulses. This part of the brain continues to develop through adolescence, therefore organizational skills are a developmental readiness issue. The middle grades student's brain is not ready to assume full responsibility in this area. Students need to see and practice the patterns of organizational behavior multiple times in nonthreatening ways. One teacher cannot provide all of the models and practices for students; a team's commitment to this task is needed.

Approaches to Take in Helping Students Develop Key Skills

1 **Take the time needed to investigate together the latest research on the adolescent brain.** Many educators graduated from college before relevant research emerged, so it was not part of their teacher preparation. Discuss how the new information impacts curriculum and instruction. Scientists are gathering fascinating information with new technology such as magnetic resonance imaging (MRI), which allows them to study how the brain functions in live subjects. This research challenges long-held beliefs and assumptions that young adolescents should be capable of managing their time effectively and able to independently follow through on long-term projects. Strong and effective teams have to be willing to study and consider information that is likely to run counter to their existing practices. Here are several resources that teams might explore:

- "Adolescent Brains Are Works in Progress" by Frontline producer Sarah Spinks www.pbs.org/wgbh/pages/frontline/shows/teenbrain/work/adolescent.html

- *Brains.org: Practical Classroom Applications of Current Brain Research* www.brains.org

- *Secrets of the Teenage Brain* by Sheryl Feinstein, www.brainstore.com

- *The Primal Teen: What New Discoveries About the Teenage Brain Tell Us About Our Kids* by Barbara Strauch (2007), Anchor Books.

Homework completion, always a huge issue, is directly connected to organizational skills. This topic often raises hackles, and conversations easily disintegrate into nonproductive grumblings. There is a lot of new research related to this issue to explore. When a team is ready to look at issues surrounding homework and take action to make homework a really effective learning strategy, they might well read together one of these books:

- *Rethinking Homework: Best Practices That Support Diverse Needs* by Cathy Vatterott (2009), ASCD. Cathy also has a website where a lot of her research is posted: www.homeworklady.com

- *Fair Isn't Always Equal* by Rick Wormeli (2006), NMSA and Stenhouse.

② **Identify specific actions that will build student organization skills and coordinate approaches to homework, long-term assignments, and organization of work.** The goal here is for teams to decide on some strategies for students to learn that will work in multiple situations. Here are a half-dozen possibilities.

- Probably the most important thing a team can agree on is what system they will use to post class and homework assignments. Some schools provide daily planners or agendas and others post everything online. Most schools fall somewhere in between. Here are a couple of simple ways to coordinate the posting of assignments:

  - Pick a place in every classroom where all of the team assignments are posted. The students can check them each morning in homeroom or advisory. Teachers can use them to prompt students to use time wisely should they finish assignments early or have some "free" time.

  - If your students are using planners or assignment notebooks, have each teacher check them in his or her class at the end of the last period of the day. Use distinctive stamps to indicate that students have gotten everything written down correctly. The stamps can be a signal to parents that the notebook has been checked. If it hasn't been stamped, parents should be encouraged to ask why not. Of course, once you include parents in this process, the team has to be faithful about checking the assignment notebooks; otherwise questioning voice mail and e-mail messages will quickly appear.

- If anyone on the team is posting assignments online, make sure everyone on the team does so. Some team members may initially need a lot of TLC to feel competent enough to use an Internet site to post information. It's embarrassing to admit one feels incompetent, and that embarrassment grows when one doesn't catch on after there is a demonstration— and then a second one. Someone who is unsure about using an online process needs a buddy who will stand by and explain the process slowly in nontechnical terms. Teammates should do that for one another.

- Teams can agree on a template for long-term assignments or projects that have multiple steps. The still-developing frontal cortex, home of the executive function, makes it highly unlikely that the vast majority of students can manage their time efficiently as they attempt to work through a multi-step assignment independently. Break down long-term assignments and projects into steps with due dates, and provide exemplars of the work. If a team uses the same basic template, then their students will have multiple practices with the same process, and they will begin to develop a pattern of behaviors. When an assignment is broken down into its components, a couple of things occur:

  - Process as well as product can be assessed.

  - Student work is more likely to be their own if the components are checked before they can move on to the next part.

  - The teacher knows when a student is confused or misguided and can step in to redirect.

64

Here's a sample template that a team might adapt and use:

Figure 4-1. Form for periodic assessment of long-term projects

Template for Assessing Component Parts of a Project

Name		Topic	
Component	Due Date	Date Completed	Planning (Teacher Initials)
Planning Steps 1. 2. 3.			
		Points earned ___	
Research Steps 1. 2. 3.			
		Points earned ___	
Creating/Drafting Steps 1. 2. 3.			
		Points earned ___	
Revising/Fine-Tuning Steps 1. 2. 3.			
		Points earned ___	
Publishing/Presenting Steps 1. 2. 3.			
		Points earned ___	
		Total points earned ___	

By chunking up the multiple steps into smaller components and giving points as each component is completed, the teacher can easily monitor student progress. The student faces a less daunting task because the components have a defined beginning and end that must be done within a relatively short span of time. This type of scaffolding is a developmentally appropriate approach to use with challenging, complex assignments.

- Help students organize their handouts, assignments, and homework with a system adaptable to the needs of each class. Using visual cues such as colors or pictures helps. For example, if the team uses folders or notebooks, red could be for language arts, blue for math, and so on. Should there be an excess of colored duplicating paper in the building, color coding handouts would also be a jazzy and effective way to help students stay organized. But alas, in most schools the colored duplicating paper is often guarded by a fire-breathing dragon and not easily accessed. Therefore, team teachers just have to be inventive. For example,

- For each subject area, pick an icon that is easily cut and pasted on teacher-made materials to help students sort and identify papers more easily. Remember, middle grades students are often entering the realm of multiple teachers with multiple expectations from a simply-organized self-contained classroom. They need help in figuring out a system that will work for them.

- This need for a good system also holds true if a school is in techno-heaven, and each child has his or her own computer. The team still needs to help students devise a system of folders on their computers to keep order. Many classrooms are almost entirely paper-free. Materials are online, assignments go into a "drop box" on the school server, or they use management systems like Moodle.

- Some schools have found great success using NoteShare Notebooks (www.aquaminds.com), software that presents itself as a spiral notebook with many unique features.

One cautionary word: whatever system the team devises, it won't work for everyone; some students will devise their own. Stay flexible and keep a sense of humor! A student may come up with an innovative system that works better for some students. Homeroom or advisory is a perfect time to have students reflect on their own organizational practices and share good ideas with one another.

- Devise a homework support system. Cathy Vatterott's research and her compilation of others' research shows that modern family life is often not in sync with teachers' homework expectations. She cites several cultural changes that teachers need to consider. The "parental dictatorship" prevalent in the mid 20th century in which children's lives were tightly controlled by their parents no longer exists for a variety of reasons. Family structures are much more diverse, and children have more power in family decisions, whether they are as simple as what to eat for dinner or more complex as where to go on family vacations. Also, modern parents' beliefs about the importance of homework are on a continuum from "schoolwork is the most important aspect of my child's life" to "it is not my job to tutor or monitor my child's schoolwork." Most families struggle to find some sort of balance in their lives between the many activities of individual family members and time spent together as a family unit. Arguments about homework put stress on these relationships. Gone for good, it seems, are the days when parents could "make" their children do their homework. Wishing for their return is not helpful, so a team needs to take the initiative in addressing this issue. Many traditional strategies for dealing with missing or poorly done homework can be tweaked to take them out of the "punishment" category and make them supportive and even ...enjoyable! One "solution" may not be the answer, but instead a creative matrix of the following alternatives may be necessary.

  - After school help: Voluntary homework clubs can be successful, especially if the team can bring in community volunteers to provide more one-on-one support for students. Approach community groups like senior citizen clubs, the Rotary, or local colleges to find helpers; having one or two extra adults in the room is extremely helpful. Make the room inviting—work in small, collaborative groups, provide healthy snacks, and come up with a clever name for this "club."

- Online support: Many teachers are finding that going online (Instant Messenger, Skype, Twitter) at a set time each evening to answer questions or provide feedback helps students immensely.

- Study groups: Set up online student study groups using IM or Skype. It's possible to have conference audio chats so two or more students could help each other. It is best to alert parents about the purpose of these groups so they are aware of what's happening. If the team isn't currently familiar with these tools, ask the students to help organize the groups and teach the teachers at the same time. Students are always going to know more about social networking than adults; it just makes sense to use their expertise. Some readers and parents may think this kind of collaboration is cheating or that some students will just copy answers. Students have been copying answers for generations, but the savvy teacher is always checking for individual understanding and soon figures out who is sharing answers and intervenes. The benefits of students working out problems collaboratively outweigh the risk of duplicitous and one-sided collaboration. If students are asked to demonstrate their new learning as an individual on a test or essay, why does it matter if they work together to initially learn the new material—how can that be "cheating"? However, we can't dismiss the issue of cheating because it is an important topic. Schools, teams, students, and parents need to have conversations about this topic and develop a common understanding of its definition to avoid recriminations and misunderstandings.

- Lunch club: Have an occasional lunch meeting to go over materials with students who are struggling or have questions.

- Morning support: Look at the team schedule. Is it possible to carve out a half hour two or three times a week for homework help? The day before at team meeting go through the list of students and decide who needs to go to the math room, who needs to go to social studies, and so on. Perhaps one teacher supervises the students who are in good shape with homework so that the other teachers can work with small groups. There are a myriad of short activities that the supervising teacher could use to enrich those students who don't need the help on that particular day—logic puzzles, creative problem solving, and improvisation. Here are some resources:

- *The Read-Aloud Handbook* by Jim Trelease
- Creative problem solving
  www.learningforlife.org/exploring/resources/99-720/x09.pd
- Improvisation activities and games:
  http://improvencyclopedia.org/games/index.html
- http://plays.about.com/od/improvgames/Improvisation_Games.htm
- Logic puzzles
  www.puzzles.com/projects/LogicProblems.html
- www.logic-puzzles.org

- Build into the schedule time for an occasional backpack and/or locker check for missing work. Students often complete assignments and then stick them somewhere "safe" and promptly forget them. Perhaps more incomprehensible to adults is students' perception that if teachers don't specifically ask for work that has missed its due date, they cannot turn it in later. Sometimes adults in the students' lives become frustrated with these behaviors, then annoyed, and possibly angry. Creating a regular organization and clean-out time saves everyone aggravation. "But," says the eighth grade teacher, "No one is going to do this for them in *high school*!" And that teacher is right. Middle grades teachers need to think systemically. Perhaps in sixth grade, the locker/backpack check takes place weekly, and in seventh grade, bi-weekly. In eighth grade, perhaps first quarter it's still bi-weekly, second quarter it is once a month, and by fourth quarter students are on their own with just reminders. Of course, there are going to be those students who need more support—the patterns of organization are just not

69

sticking. Don't get mad, just them send them regularly to their lockers with a pass, a trashcan, and a good friend who can help them sort through the jumble.

Let's be honest here. Almost every team has one of its own who is organizationally challenged and struggles to keep her own desk and paperwork straight. Her desk can be identified by leaning towers of handouts or by complex arrays of files on the laptop desktop. (I plead guilty—colleagues still make jokes about my desk and now my desktop!) Despite great intentions to utilize the team's system, such a teammate may need some support. Therefore, it's important that the team takes time to discuss which strategies they all can commit to and follow through on. It is better to work together on one strategy well than announce to students that everyone is going to do X, Y, and Z in every class and then have those plans disintegrate. That's poor modeling and will undermine the entire purpose of helping students understand that organizational strategies are useful and necessary. Also when team commitments fall by the wayside, tensions can develop that undermine team cohesiveness. The KISS principle (Keep It Simple, Stupid!) is a mantra worth repeating at every team meeting!

Help Students Develop Organizational Skills by...

1 **Posting cues for students in the team area and online; model and practice with them behaviors that promote lifelong learning.** These actions will help students refocus on expectations, processes, and procedures when their attention wanders elsewhere.

- **Use doorway reminders.** "I don't have a pencil!" "Did we need that book today?" How many classes begin with these exclamations? Teachers are thinking, "How could you forget your textbook?" Students had good intentions, but somehow between first period and second period and 20 feet of hallway, they've lost all writing utensils and the ability to anticipate what they need for class. It's that pesky immature executive function in the brain's frontal lobes that is failing to keep the young adolescent well organized and prepared for class. Seventh grade teams at Mt. Ararat Middle School in Topsham, Maine, and many others across the country came up with a simple solution. Each teacher uses a small white board to list materials needed for class and places it on a chair at the entrance of the classroom. Students can do a last minute scan of the list of the needed materials, do a double-check of what they have in hand, and make a quick dash to their lockers to grab an errant math book. This strategy is a simple way to provide reminders to students, and who knows—perhaps it will also start to build patterns of being prepared for class. When schools move, as they are, to each child having his or her own computer, many of the issues disappear because everything—texts, writing implements, homework—are all encompassed in the device.

Figure 4-2. Teachers at Fossum Middle School, McAllen, TX, post reminders for students.

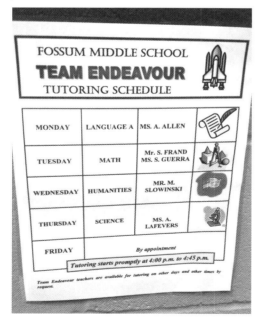

- **Create locker/team area posters.** Is there a big project with multiple steps underway? A test scheduled? Create amusing posters that give specific actions cuing students to what they should be doing to complete the project or prepare for the test. Computers make it so easy to create colorful, eye catching posters to place around the team area, on lockers, and even in the bathrooms. If none of the teachers have time to create these posters—find a student who enjoys graphic design or cartoon making to design the posters.

Figure 4-3. Create posters with actions students must take to complete an assignment.

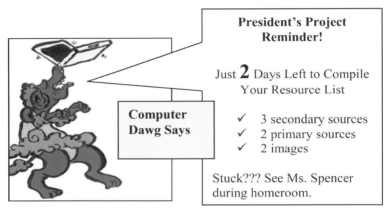

Cartoon figure created by Andrew Greenstone, Creative Commons License

In a one-to-one computing environment, teachers can send reminders to students via e-mail or on a class wiki, and students can easily ask questions using these formats.

- **Generate checklists.** Generate with the students a morning and an afternoon checklist that can be posted in their lockers. The easiest process, of course, is just to manufacture the list and hand it out on the first day of school. However, the students have no ownership of the teachers' list, and it quickly will become invisible. A more useful process is to allow students to produce the list. Here's an Extended Think-Pair-Share application that results in a class list generated by students.

Figure 4-4. Activity: Extended Think-Pair-Share

Making a Class List by Consensus

1. Have each student create a list of the five most important things to do at the beginning of the day. It's important to put it in writing because each student will be sharing it with another.

2. Pair up the group and have each pair compare and discuss their lists before writing a new one of five items combining the most important items from each list.

3. Then each pair joins another pair. They share and discuss their lists. The group of four then collaborates on a list with which they all agree. Because there is a limit on the number of items, students really need to ponder and negotiate. Having no limit might just lead to a combining of lists until it becomes unwieldy and useless.

4. Each foursome joins another foursome. They share and discuss their lists. The group of eight then collaborates on a list of five on which they all agree.

5. As the groups get larger, the teacher should carefully monitor time and conversations. If groups get bogged down, the teacher can do a bit of coaching.

6. Depending on the time frame the class has for this process, keep combining groups to further refine the lists. The ultimate goal is to continue combining until there is just one really good list. Sometimes time constraints prevent this outcome.

7. At whatever point the process ends, chart and duplicate the "ultimate" list and have students post it in their locker or their notebooks. Naturally this process could be done digitally with the resulting list sent to all the students for keeping on their desktops and the class wiki.

8. The process can't stop here! During the first couple of weeks of school build in time to have students check the list to see if they have everything they need. Building patterns of behaviors takes time initially, but the payoff comes later when behaviors become automatic, and time is spent on class work rather than rounding up supplies.

- **Teach students a common note taking strategy that will work across the curriculum.** A major organizational behavior for students is taking good notes, keeping them in an orderly fashion, and knowing how to use them for learning. By using a common strategy students receive plenty of opportunity to practice the process and build some proficiency that the teachers in the next grade level can build on. One of the best methods is Cornell style (http://coe.jmu.edu/learningtoolbox/cornellnotes.html). Cornell notes have three sections: notes, review words and questions, and a summary. Students draw a straight line down the left side of their notebook paper making about 2.5- to 3-inch margin. The notes go on the right-hand side. After note taking is done, the students review the notes for key words and ideas and write them on the left-hand side. Then students write a summary statement at the bottom. Here's a sample focusing on types of volcanoes.

Figure 4-5. Example of Cornell notes

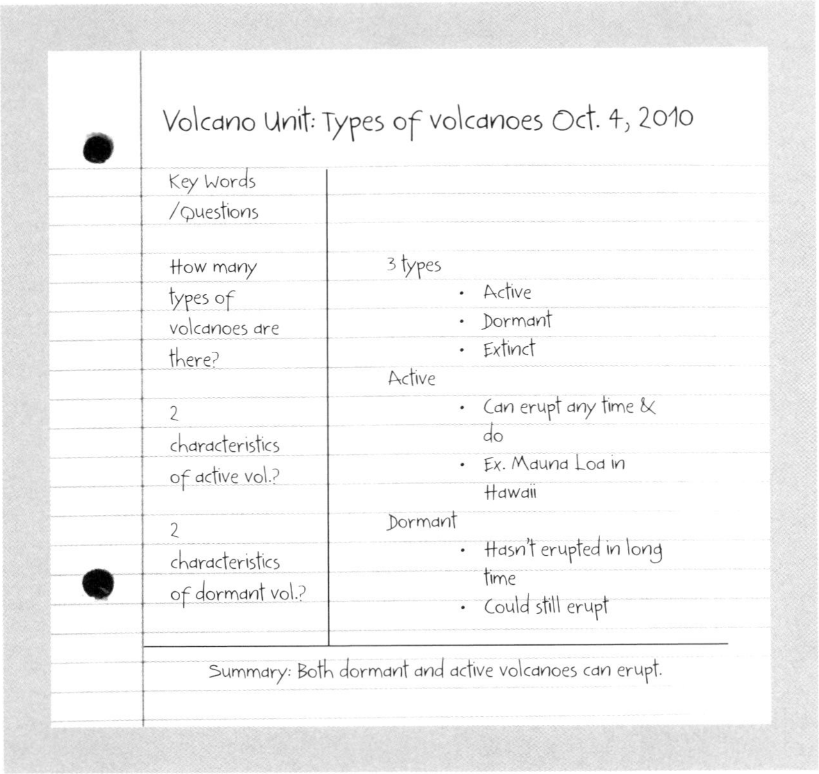

The really cool characteristic of Cornell notes is that students have a reason and a way to review their notes. The teacher leaves time at the end of the lesson for students to review their notes and to write the key word and questions in the left-hand margin. Then the students can literally crease their paper along the margin line and look at just the key words and question side and quiz themselves. Team teachers can help each other out by taking time in homeroom or advisory to have students review their notes regularly.

For the many students now regularly using laptops for schoolwork, it is still possible to take notes digitally using the Cornell setup. One easy way is to set up a table in either a Word document or a Google Docs document. Have students configure a table like that shown in Figure 4-6 below. Students write their notes in the right column and their review words and questions in the left column.

Figure 4-6. *Cornell notes formatted for the computer*

Key Words and Questions	Notes
How many types of volcanoes are there?	3 types • Active • Dormant • Extinct
2 characteristics of active volcanoes?	Active • Can erupt any time & do • Ex. Mauna Loa in Hawaii
2 characteristics of dormant volcanoes?	Dormant • Hasn't erupted in long time • Could still erupt

Although the digital page cannot be creased for the self-quiz, students could create temporary opaque text boxes to hide their notes while they look at just the left-hand side of the page. It's easy to click and drag a text box to check the answers. Ask the students for ideas about doing Cornell notes digitally—they are always a terrific source of digital solutions.

Learning to take notes is one of those skills that most students see as real drudgery; therefore, finding ways to create a little bit of fun is useful. Or as Mary Poppins said, "A spoonful of sugar makes the medicine go down..." Some ideas include

- Hold contests with prizes for the best review questions.

- Add a column for student-created images that help explain ideas.

- Use props or costumes to keep students' attention.

- Stop every seven or eight minutes and allow students to check with each other to fill in any missing information.

- Make use of the fantastic video clips on the Web that will illustrate the main points of your lesson. If YouTube and other video sites are blocked at school, here's what to do. At home go to the video site, copy the URL, and then go to www.zamzar.com/ This site will convert the video to a .mov file allowing you to download it to your home computer. Then you can email it to yourself at school or burn a CD with the video on it. Be sure to check the restrictions on the video site because some require that only their site be used to view the video. Make sure students have the URL so they can go back and check the video explanation whenever they need a second, third, or fourth look.

Be aware that a portion of any population has great difficulty taking notes for a variety of reasons. They may not be able to look at an overhead and transfer the words to their own paper, or they may be auditory processors and need to just listen. Knowing the students and their specific learning needs is crucial if teams are going to help them internalize the organizational skills necessary for life-long learning. No one note taking approach is fail proof, and adjustments and modifications will need to occur. Students need a lot of support and a chance to see many, many models of what good notes look like.

- **Plant the seed of the value of study groups.** Some readers will remember the old movie and television show *The Paper Chase*, which focused on a group of law students. Having so much information to master that it was nearly impossible to do it independently, they banded together to help each other succeed, and much of the film's action took place in their study group. Teaching middle grades students this approach to learning makes sense and builds on their natural inclination to be with peers. Teams should be creative in finding time for study groups to work together. Here are some suggestions:

    - Provide time during homeroom or advisory for students to compare class notes. They can clarify vague information, add details, and correct inaccurate information. Needless to say, teachers should model what these groups might say and do; it is not enough to merely provide the time. The team teachers also need to monitor and coach the groups and help students understand that they do no one a favor by simply allowing a friend to copy word-for-word. Study groups provide a perfect opening for discussions about personal integrity and responsibility. If homeroom is too short, a team might consider extending homeroom by ten minutes to allow students time to experience study groups once or twice a week.

    - Set up study groups at school that operate online after school. Many students already use some form of instant messaging with audio and video applications plus conference call capacity. Because this is new territory for most teachers and parents, it needs to be done with a lot of thought. Including parents and administrators in the planning is necessary so that everyone is aware of the parameters. Also spend time with students to help them understand the possibilities and the responsibilities accompanying digital communication. Young adolescents find it difficult to distinguish the line between just telling someone the answer and helping him or her understand the process of finding the answer. A good discussion topic for advisory or a parent group would be "What's the difference between collaboration and cheating?"

Using key words like "working together on homework" or "collaboration + cheating" send the searcher to some interesting blog posts that could stimulate conversations. Also worth exploring are online sites that help set up online study groups. Google "online study groups" to locate possibilities. As with any online work, the user needs to fully investigate the levels of available security. Online opportunities for collaboration are not going to diminish, only multiply. Teams and schools cannot bury their heads in the sand and hope they won't intrude into their space. Instead, it is important to learn how to use them to benefit students and their learning.

- **Plan time for students to regularly review their class notes.** Students are expected to maintain notebooks or laptop files and keep class notes and other materials in an orderly fashion. For generations teachers have exhorted students to review their materials nightly rather than cramming for exams. For generations students have ignored that advice and crammed the night before the big test. Students learn to value what teachers spend time on, and if no time is spent on learning how to learn, then students won't spend the time practicing those skills either. If reviewing material is a worthwhile habit to acquire, then teachers should provide time to build that habit. In her book *How to Teach Students to Remember*, Marilee Sprenger emphasizes that review should not be left for the end of the unit but should be ongoing. Teams can help build this organizational habit by building in time regularly to stop and review, or possibly use one of these two means:

- **Begin each class with a review of the previous lesson.** The time will be well spent for several reasons:

  - It focuses students on the work of the day—it brings their mental concentration out of the hallway and into the classroom.

  - It clues in students who were absent the day before to the work at hand.

  - It reveals misconceptions or gaps students have and provides teachers with critical information to help shape the day's lesson (formative assessment).

- **Set a schedule** for homeroom/advisory such as Monday, social studies review and Tuesday, science review. Each teacher provides his or her teammates with a simple two- or three-minute review scenario, and each homeroom teacher can report where there seem to be problems. Using this process also sends the message to the students that all of the teachers care about how they are doing in all of their classes.

- **Consider setting up a team wiki.** Google "middle school" + "team wiki" and examples of middle grades wikis from all over the world pop up. They are all different in organization and graphics, but they provide students with important information that they can access 24/7. There are varying views of how much access to their wiki a team should give their students. It can vary from read-only access only all the way to everyone on the team having writing privileges. It's easy to begin with the originators exercising lots of control. As their comfort level grows, teams may feel that they want to make the wiki more interactive. Here are just some of the ways teams are using wikis:

  - List assignments
  - List resources
  - Showcase exemplary student work
  - Share calendars
  - Recognize students, parents, and community members for contributions
  - Share pictures
  - FAQs
  - Make school activities transparent.

Many educators subscribe to the gradual-release-of-responsibility model that calls for the responsibility for following through on a multi-stepped task to fall more and more on students until they can complete them independently. A team may only have one year with students, but if they think about that year longitudinally in terms of developing organizational and learning skills in their students, they have the opportunity to help student build habits that will last them a lifetime.

Also, think about ways to include the allied arts teachers in this process. E-mail makes it easy to share assignments that can be posted in homerooms and on wikis. Share assessment lists, rubrics, and checklists with colleagues in the allied arts, and negotiate ways they can be used in both team classes and allied arts classes. Help students prepare for allied arts exams or assessments in homeroom or study times. Yes, this is an extra effort and takes time. However, if the team's mission revolves around student learning, then these efforts are fully justified.

2 **Teach students to always have a Plan B.** One key to staying organized and being prepared is to always have a fallback plan. If your car doesn't start in morning, whom will you call? You back up your files in case your hard drive crashes. If your lesson plan flops for your sub, you have puzzles and read–alouds available. For adults, having a Plan B is often second nature. Young adolescents, especially ones who have had everything done for them as youngsters, often don't know what to do if something goes awry. Nancy Rideout, a teacher in Sabattus, Maine, teaches her fifth graders about Plan Bs from the first days of school. "You don't have a pencil, go to Plan B." When she receives blank stares, she takes time to brainstorm with her class all of the possibilities—borrow one from a friend, look around on the floor, use a marker until you can get one. "What's your Plan B if you leave your homework assignment at school?" She doesn't get angry with them, but instead offers them a way to solve the problem on their own. Within a very short time, her students catch on and are eager to share with her how they implemented a Plan B. "I forgot to write down my assignment, Ms. Rideout, but I figured out Plan B–I called Michelle." Her praise for their effort reinforces a positive behavior, and students begin to understand that they have both the responsibility and the power to figure out solutions to troublesome situations that crop up. Now, take one teacher's action and magnify it to an all-team approach to problem solving organizational blips. If in every class students are cheerfully asked to devise Plan Bs, they will probably become adept at it. It can lead to some highly creative thinking.

- *Because the server's down, we can't use the computers for research, and the library is full. What can we do for a plan B?* We could interview each other about what we've already found out and share information!

- *Because there's a leak in the gym, we can't play volleyball during activity time—what should our Plan B be?* Do you have any balloons? We could play fingertip balloon volleyball right here in the room.

Empowering students to figure out how to solve minor problems will build their capacity to solve bigger ones as they come along. Flexible thinking is an important part of the learning process.

Some students are fortunate to have homes that come equipped with a quiet study space and an adult ready and able to help with school work. Many, many do not. A team should be proactive and help students develop Plan Bs to address out-of-school work.

- You're at home, stuck on assignment, and don't know what to do?

    - Who can you call?
    - Is there an online resource that might help? www. infoplease.com/homework
    - If you find no solution, what will you say to the teacher the next day? What solution will you suggest? Some teams plan for this contingency and have a form for students to fill out that calls for the student to describe next steps to get the work done. When a student fills it out and follows through, there are no penalties. Figure 4-7 is an example of such a form.

- Is there a time and place where you can go right after school that is quiet so you can work?

- Is there a way to get to school early to work?

- What might you say to your teacher to negotiate a different approach?

Figure 4-7. Student form describing steps for completing late homework

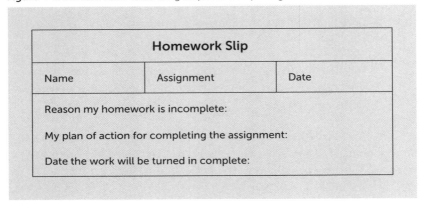

- You have no supplies for a project.

  - What are your alternatives? Is it possible to complete the project on a school computer?

  - How might you approach your teacher to ask if you can borrow markers and other supplies? Many teams are recognizing that there is a real uneven playing field when it comes to projects. Because many families just do not have the money to go buy foam boards or fancy computer graphic programs, all projects are completed during school time using school supplies. When schools achieve the goal of each child having his or her own laptop, the playing field will be level. Each child will have access to high quality resources and presentation software and thus will not suffer from an economic handicap in pursuit of an education.

Even though it isn't measured on standardized tests, learning to develop Plan Bs when their organization skills come up short and leave them without a pencil or book is a good use of students' time, because it develops that all-important critical thinking skill.

3 **With students write a standard and assessment list or rubric for organization.** Send a message to students and parents that organization skills are key to learning and achievement by taking time to write a standard and grade level indicators for organization and study skills with the students. As already pointed out, if these skills are truly valued and accepted as key to lifelong learning, then real time and not just lip service must be given to modeling and practicing these skills. A standard states the goal unequivocally, and students and parents are clear about what being an organized fifth, sixth, seventh, or eighth grader looks like. A team might revamp the schedule for a week early in the year and block out 30 minutes a day to work through this process in homeroom or advisory groups. The process should include these components:

- Brainstorm the critical elements of 'being organized" for a middle school student.

- Use content area standards as models.

- Break students into small groups to write a standard and indicators. Share and have students revise.

- Choose a small group of students to review all the possibilities, and have them narrow the list down to a small number.

- Have students democratically choose their standard for organization.

- Coach the process to help students consider all of the important elements.

- Share the final product with parents.

- Have students regularly reflect on how they are doing with sharpening their organizational skills. Perhaps these reflections can be part of the students' portfolios.

A last word
from Jill...

Organizational skills, seemingly intuitive in some students, can be and should be learned by everyone. However, it's wise to remember that just like an 80-pound sixth grader cannot hoist 150-pound barbells, most young adolescent brains are not ready to assume the heavy lifting of managing their busy lives without help from a variety of sources. It's also important to remember that today's young adolescents' lives are much busier and more heavily scheduled than those who grew up 20 years ago. There is more for them to manage. Scaffolding, not haranguing, will develop good habits and practices over time.

5

Design a Cross-Curricular Literacy Program

As students move through the middle grades, the reading and writing requirements become more diverse and complex. New skills need to be learned and others updated. When teams collaborate in meeting this need, each child's skills will continue to develop effectively.

Ella's Day

5:45-6:00 a.m.: The alarm goes off. Opening her laptop, Ella checks her Facebook page to see whether she missed anything overnight. She responds to a friend and then switches to her IM account where she sends a message to find out what her friend Shareese is wearing to school.

6:45-7:20 a.m.: She grabs a bagel on her way out the door while texting on her phone. She continues to text on the bus while scanning her assignment notebook to make sure she has completed her homework.

7:30-7:50 a.m.: While in homeroom she rereads her essay for language arts on her school laptop making a few minor revisions and then tries to sneak in an IM to a friend in another homeroom. Busted! Her teacher admonishes her to stick to schoolwork on the laptop.

8:00-9:15 a.m.: In science class Ella and her lab partner need to revise the conclusion section of their lab report. They didn't provide enough evidence to support their statements. Later, the class is asked to go to an Internet site on adaptation. The teacher sets the purpose for reading and the gives the students a graphic organizer to help them take notes on the main ideas. The site has some vocabulary Ella doesn't know, but fortunately those words are mostly hyperlinked to an explanation, so she understands most of what she is reading. The students are asked to write a summary of the big ideas as a Ticket Out the Door.

9:20-10:35 a.m.: Phys Ed—volley ball

10:40-11:10 a.m.: Back in homeroom for silent sustained reading, Ella has discovered graphic novels and has scheduled a reading conference with her teacher.

11:15-12:00 p.m.: Lunch and recess. Ella is very good at keeping her phone hidden while texting so that she doesn't get caught breaking the school's no-phone rule.

12:05-1:20 p.m.: After reviewing the math homework, the teacher directs the students to their textbooks. The students read two pages of text and look at several graphs and charts in preparation for the teacher's lecture. After the teacher's explanation, students work on the assignment that includes several lengthy word problems. At the end of class, Ella and her classmates pull out their math journals and write an explanation of the process they used to solve one of the problems.

1:25-2:40 p.m.: In social studies class Ella and her partner are reading a primary source document from colonial days. They struggle with the funny-shaped letters and different syntax. They prepare a chart to share that summarizes what their document said.

2:45-3:15 p.m.: Ella texts with friends during the bus ride home.

3:45-5:00p.m. Swim practice—no phones in the pool!

7:00-9:30 p.m. Homework time. In between IMing and checking Facebook and an occasional Tweet, Ella reads two chapters of a book and responds to a prompt on the class wiki. She also does some Internet research for her social studies project on the Massachusetts Bay Colony. She cuts and pastes important information into her notes folder. She then practices paraphrasing those notes because she understands that she just can't use someone else's words in her project. She's trying to understand the concept of plagiarism. She finishes up by answering questions for science class based on the graphic organizer they did in class.

9:30 p.m. Until her parents say "lights out" she is social networking and and writing a movie review at www.kidreviewer.com

Lights out, but Ella is under the covers with a flashlight composing a poem about the dreamy guy who sits next to her in social studies.

Middle grades students like Ella have many rich reading and writing experiences in the course of a day, and not all are assigned by teachers. These experiences require far more diverse and complex skills than the literacy instruction in elementary school provided. Becoming literate is a developmental process, and students need to learn new skills and update others all the way through high school, perhaps even into college. When middle grades teams approach this need in a systematic way, their students will continue to develop the sophisticated reading and writing skills they need to be successful in middle school and beyond.

Working Together to Improve Students' Reading and Writing is Critically Important Because...

1 **The middle grades curriculum requires that students read and write more complex materials.** Furthermore, as these content materials become more sophisticated, the skills needed to be proficient in each discipline are not all the same. Reading a science text is quite different from reading a novel. Students need instruction from the content experts, their content teachers, on how to read and write as a scientist, an historian, or a health professional. However, many content teachers have little training in applying literacy skills to their teaching so it's sensible to collaborate with the language arts and reading teachers on their team to learn some effective strategies. Figure 5-1 shows a couple of examples that illustrate the differences among the disciplines.

2 **Many reading/writing skills are common across the curriculum.** Examples include writing constructed responses, navigating Internet sites, and understanding the protocols of persuasion. Having a coordinated plan ensures that students strive to meet similar expectations across the curriculum and have opportunities for lots of practice.

Figure 5-1. *Differences in Literacy Standards Across the Curriculum*

	Language Arts	Math	Science
Reading	Understand the role of conflict, setting, character development, and theme	Understand text that is dense in concepts	Make sense of technical directions and diagrams
Writing	Analyze poetry and offer original thoughts about the content	Make connections between the past and present	Explain how scientific processes are used in a lab

3 **It is impossible for one teacher to provide all-inclusive instruction and practice in the myriad of reading and writing skills young adolescents need.** This task calls for a team effort. Plus everyone (students and teachers) benefits if students are better equipped to read and write for a variety of purposes. Furthermore, as researchers Daniel Willingham (2009) and Robert Marzano (2004) point out, background knowledge is critical to comprehension, especially in making inferences. Because literacy skills do not develop in a vacuum, students need a rich learning environment. Students build background knowledge about the world in their content classes, and, working together, team teachers can widen students' knowledge by planning special events and experiences. Although teachers have no control over what students experience outside of school, a crucial everyday role of middle grades teams is to combine skill development with an engaging and meaningful curriculum that explores all aspects of real-world events. Visit Daniel Willingham's website www.danielwillingham.com and view his short video *Teaching Content Is Teaching Reading* for a quick overview of the connection between background knowledge and comprehension.

Next Steps
to Take

1 **Identify those practices in reading and writing that are common in your classrooms.** One really smart move to help with this is to adopt the reading specialist in your building. Entice this expert with candy to come to team meetings regularly. Two other people to shower with goodies are the librarian and the technology integrator. These people will help the team quickly identify key skills to concentrate on, teach the team how to implement the strategies to teach these key skills, and help teachers locate and use resources such as lexiles, trade books, and Internet sites. Some readers are thinking—"Hmmmm, we don't have any specialists or any staff development in literacy—what can we do?" Here are two sites with a wealth of information on locating resources.

- www.readwritethink.org
- www.litandlearn.lpb.org/strategies.html

Beyond adopting the school's literacy experts, a team can agree to observe the easy-to-implement practices shown in Figures 5-2 through 5-5 that are effective in building student literacy proficiencies.

Figure 5-2.

Team practices for building literacy—Reading

1. Build prior knowledge before assigning a text to help students begin building mental maps of important concepts:
   - Show pictures/videos related to text.
   - Introduce key vocabulary.
   - Ask students what they already know about the topic.
2. Set a purpose for reading to help students focus their efforts:
   - Be specific "Read to find four reasons why..."
   - Write the purpose on the board or chart paper so students can refer to it as they read.

3. Give students time to talk about the text in small groups to clarify their thinking:
   - Stop after five minutes of reading and do a think-pair-share.
   - Allow students to rehearse ideas orally in small groups before asking them to respond in writing.
4. Ask students to reflect on what is important to remember from their reading:
   - "What connections can you make between what we read today and our time?
   - "Why do you think the author chose to...?"
   - "What questions do you still have?"
   - "What do you think are the most important ideas? Most interesting?"

By adhering to these four simple procedures, teachers provide practice in several of the behaviors that good readers do automatically and less able readers rarely do independently. The team is building good reading habits in their students. Likewise, your team should decide on practices for building students' writing proficiency.

Figure 5-3.

Team Practices for Building Writing Proficiency

- Use common language when talking about writing. Is the initial attempt at writing a first *draft* or a *sloppy copy*, and what do those words actually mean—when do we worry about spelling, complete sentences, etc.? Make sure that each teacher means the same thing when using the terms *revision* and *editing*. Too often students receive mixed messages about terminology and get frustrated when they have misinterpreted a teacher's direction. Naturally, it would really be useful if the entire school, not just the team, used the same terminology!

- Discuss and agree on the importance of writing to learning and the way that the team will approach writing. Some teams actually prepare and sign an agreement that spells out their plan. See an example in Figure 5-4.

Figure 5-4.

Team Writing Plan

- We will give our students multiple opportunities for writing and will follow a process writing model. *(In other words, no teacher will simply assign a written product, have student write it at home, collect it the next day, and mark it for errors, etc.)*

- We will use *writing to learn strategies* in each of our classes on a weekly basis to help students reinforce concepts and skills in class.

- We will give students frequent opportunities for writing projects in all content areas. These written projects will take a variety of forms.

- We will collaborate with one another as we identify writing problems and help students eliminate these problems to become clearer thinkers and writers.

- We will develop and use team rubrics for common writing tasks.

- Students will be encouraged to revise and resubmit unacceptable written work until it is high quality work.

- Students will be encouraged to use their laptops for all phases of the writing process.

  - Adapted from "Whole Language on a Team" in Dickinson and Erb, eds.(1997).

Teach students that digital text requires the application of additional strategies beyond those they use with a textbook or other print source. The research is beginning to come in on the differences between reading print and digital text. Dr. Don Leu and the New Literacies Research Team at the University of Connecticut are among the leaders exploring the impact of the digital world on traditional literacy practice. Carol Duffy, a teacher from Lamoine, Maine, participated in a research project directed by Leu. When asked how her practice had changed as a result of this experience, Duffy highlighted several things (personal communication, January 3, 2010).

- No longer is she the sole provider of the Internet sites her students use. She has found that it is important to teach them how to find sites and to evaluate them for reliability. Earlier generations did not need to think about the reliability of the information they were reading. *World Book, Britannica*, and other publishers vetted the information before it ever made it to the library shelf. No longer— it really is a "consumer beware!" world on the World Wide Web. Students need to become informed and discriminating consumers of information. Fortunately the Web also provides the tools and information to help Internet users become savvy consumers. Good resources include:

  - http://novemberlearning.com/Resources/Information Literacy Resources

  - www.lib.berkeley.edu/Help/guides.html UC Berkeley Library

  - http://school.discoveryeducation.com/schrockguide Kathy Schrock's site. Click on Internet Information in the menu under *Subject Access*

- Duffy also follows Leu's recommendation to assign students to work in groups, usually a triad, when using Internet resources. She poses questions that require students to search, evaluate, and understand information at a variety of sites. Modifying the traditional think-pair-share strategy to explore allows her students to search on their own and then share resources. Students also participate in chat rooms set up by Duffy to share information and resources, ask questions, and discuss findings. When asked how she monitors what goes on in the chat rooms, Duffy shared that she is also a participant in the chat and, most importantly, she uses her two feet and is always up and about checking and coaching. Duffy is fortunate that StudyWiz (www.studywiz.com), a virtual learning environment, is part of the Maine Learning Technology Initiative available to all seventh and eighth graders across the state. However, teachers elsewhere are experimenting with online tools like Chatz (www.chatzy.com) or Moodle (http://moodle.org) to provide their students an opportunity to have digital conversations about their work.

- The third way her practice has changed is in the area of written communication. To her writing curriculum, she has added additional lessons on voice and purpose and how they pertain to e-mail and other online communication tools. Since she communicates with her students through e-mail, she also is teaching them the responsibilities that accompany the ability to connect instantaneously.

Figure 5-5.

Team Plan for Digital Text

- Teach students how to find a variety of sites and how to evaluate them for reliability.
- Have students work in groups (usually triads) when using Internet resources.
- Have students search on their own and then share resources.
- Always be on the move checking and coaching.
- Encourage students to have digital conversations about their work.
- Provide lessons on how to communicate by e-mail and the responsibilities involved.

2 **Create a simple plan for addressing key literacy skills that span the curriculum areas.** On a year's calendar, map out who will introduce what skills and how they will be reinforced in other classes. Connect the plan to units already being taught. Use available data to identify where the gaps in literacy are for the present year's students. For example, if most students don't really understand inferential thinking, where is the first place in the curriculum that students are expected to make inferences? That unit, that lesson—no matter what subject area—is a good place to plug in direct instruction on inferential thinking. Next step: figure out where to reinforce the original instruction. Students need lots of practice in different venues to master a skill. Here is an example of how to make such a calendar and what it might look like.

To make the calendar

1. A team identifies the critical skills they feel impact most of their classes. For example, a team might conclude the following are the skills their students most need to practice.

   - Reading: Using the parts of a textbook, setting a purpose for reading, identifying the main idea and supporting details, interacting with text by asking questions, making inferences, and synthesizing information from several sources.

   - Writing: open-ended responses, using evidence to support an idea, paragraph organization, journal responses, and persuasion.

2. Then they place them in the calendar as shown in Figure 5-6 on the following page.

This particular example of mapping literacy strategies is not meant as the perfect scope and sequence of adolescent literacy, but simply illustrates that teams can plan and work together to reinforce those literacy skills in their curriculum areas that will have far reaching benefits for their students beyond their present grade level.

Because teachers are under considerable pressure to cover specific materials, often within a restrictive and non-educationally-sound pacing guide, the idea of adding more to do within a class period is daunting. However, it's important to say once again that the advancing complexity of curriculum expectations in the middle grades and the unwritten standards of real life require that continuous attention be paid to teaching literacy skills. Furthermore, students need to see the content area experts modeling these skills within the context of the disciplines. When team teachers consciously plan how they will collaboratively address these literacy skills and use time efficiently and with purpose, the task becomes much less daunting.

Figure 5-6. Calendar of Team Teaching Reading and Writing Skills

September	October	November	December	January
Language Arts: short open-ended response **Math & SS:** study organization of the textbook and how to use the parts	**SS & Science:** reinforce short open-ended responses **Language Arts:** set a purpose for reading **Math:** reinforce use of a textbook by using glossaries	**SS:** reinforce short open-ended responses **Science:** reinforce setting a purpose for reading by identifying cause and effect organization in text **Language Arts:** Identify main idea and supporting detail Students review and reflect on their literacy portfolios	**SS:** reinforce identifying main ideas and supporting details **Science:** write cause & effect explanations in open-ended responses **Math:** reinforce setting a purpose for reading by deconstructing word problems to understand structure and task. **Language Arts:** persuasive text	**SS & Science:** read persuasive texts **Math:** introduce journals as a way for students to explore how they think when solving problems. **Language Arts:** write the persuasive essay

February	March	April	May	June
SS, Science & Math: asking questions while reading text–digital & print **Language Arts:** direct instruction on making inferences and using reading journals/wikis to practice explaining the thought processes students are using when making inferences	**Math:** Self-assess math journals and set goal to improve **SS:** continue to work on asking questions while reading, emphasizing higher level and open ended questions **Science:** quick writes where students take a stand and write to persuade **Language Arts:** explore paragraph organization through purpose	Students review and reflect on their literacy portfolios Interdisciplinary unit where everyone is working on synthesizing and organizing information for a presentation whose purpose is to persuade.		Students review their portfolios for a final reflection on their growth in the following areas: • Journal writing • Short open-ended responses • Being persuasive • Comprehending complex text

Strategies That Work

1 **Model, model, model! Model thinking when reading content material and model thinking when writing.** Metacognition, thinking about thinking, is one of the key elements in how people learn. Students see strategies in action that they can try out when they are reading or writing when they observe their teachers

- Working their way through a text.
- Asking questions.
- Using specific strategies to decode tough vocabulary words.
- Think aloud about how they will approach writing assignments.

Modeling strategies is a powerful teaching tool, especially when coupled with guided practice and feedback to students. Modeling sounds easy, however, a couple of components will make it more engaging and useful to students.

- Use mesmerizing text. Most textbooks are boriiiiiiiiiing! There are so many fascinating resources on the Internet that there is no excuse to use a deadly, dull text. Hooking the students with good content keeps them attentive as the teacher demonstrates a particular reading strategy. Even if a teacher doesn't have access to a LCD projector, it is easy to download documents and make transparencies of them. It's important to have the text up on the screen so that everyone can follow along as features are pointed out. Make sure that the text is large enough for the student in the last row to read it easily from the screen.

- Use the gradual-release-of-responsibility model. As the lesson advances, the teacher gradually turns more of the work over to the students. The model progresses through four steps: I do it! We do it! You do it together! And finally, You do it alone! (Frey and Fisher, p.7).

- Rehearse. Know what examples will be used and what steps need to occur. Anticipate what parts of the text might confuse the students, and plan concrete ways for them to deal with these challenging sections.

- Ask for student advice when modeling how to approach a writing assignment. Young adolescents love to give advice, and this interaction will help keep them engaged in the lesson.

- Keep a collection of student-generated writing assignments for use as exemplars or for analysis. Modeling and metacognitive thinking do not always have to be done by the teacher. Allowing students to analyze exemplars to identify what makes the piece outstanding gives students ownership of the process. It's no longer the teacher-as-expert saying, "This is what makes this paper good," but rather the students become the experts by labeling the critical attributes.

2 **Use the same rubrics and assessment lists in all of the classes for writing and projects.** Open-ended responses, journals, persuasive essays, reports, and digital presentations all share common elements across the curriculum. Teachers can add additional elements that refer to their specific content requirements. Common expectations send very clear messages to students: "This may be social studies, but you are expected to use Standard English conventions. They are just as important here as in language arts." Content teachers often immediately respond, "Wait—I don't want to teach grammar." Unfortunately too many adults flash back to their own papers in high school covered in red corrections, and they begin to shudder and hyperventilate. The expectation isn't that the math or science teachers become grammarians but rather that they hold all students to a standard of high quality work and accepted usages that they themselves practice. Anyone qualified to teach is able to recognize *"Them planarian has gots a three-branched instine"* as substandard work and should require students to revise. Turnabout is fair play, of course, and the math teacher should expect that the language arts teacher could help students find the average or mean of their grades.

Sometimes an assessment list is easier and faster to generate than a well-written rubric. See Figure 5-7 for open-ended responses modeled on Anne Davies' work (http://annedavies.com)

Figure 5-7.

Open Ended Response Assessment List

Parts	Met	Next Steps
Opening Sentence		
• addresses question	_____	
• clearly states position or main idea	_____	
Evidence		
• cites supporting details from text	_____	
• makes connections	_____	
• self to text	_____	
• text to text	_____	
• text to world	_____	
• information is specific & accurate	_____	
• information is organized in a way that is easy for the reader to follow	_____	
• uses the appropriate vocabulary	_____	
Concluding Sentence		
• restates main idea	_____	
• succinct & to the point	_____	
Spelling & Grammar		
• errors do not distract from reader's understanding	_____	

This format is especially useful because it provides spaces for the teacher or peer editor to list very specific steps the writer should take to meet the criteria.

Using a similar assessment strategy across team classes also helps students improve the quality of their work because they have a consistent target to aim for. Here's a variation of a strategy called Traffic Light developed by assessment guru Dylan Wiliam and his colleagues (Leahy, Lyon, Thompson, and Wiliam, 2005). Students receive red, yellow, and green dots or use similarly colored markers or pens. When peer editing or assessing, they use the green dots to indicate the parts of the piece that meet the standards described on the assessment list or rubric, yellow dots to show the parts that are close but still need some work, and red ones to mark those sections that do not meet standards. Students also jot down or share specific suggestions for improvement.

Posting these assessments lists or rubrics along with exemplars on the team webpage or wiki provides support for students and parents. Students have the assessment list that they left back in their lockers, and parents have examples to use when discussing the quality of the work with their children. It is also good for public relations with the community. When someone starts to complain that the school has low standards, one can simply call up the appropriate site on a computer or smart phone and say, "Well, let's take a look at what we expect from students. How close are these examples of exemplary work to your expectations? This is our goal for all of our students." Evidence of good work presented in a respectful way deflates criticism and turns it into admiration.

3 **Remember that reading is a social activity. Interacting with others about text helps the reader think more deeply.**
Providing time for students to talk about what they are reading while they are reading helps them practice comprehension skills such as asking questions, summarizing, and making connections to other experiences. Think how often students get to the end of piece of text and turn to their teacher and say, "I don't get it!" Many middle grades students have not yet developed the skills to self-monitor their reading so that they can quickly identify when they are getting confused. Nor are they able to independently retrieve and use strategies that might help them work through the confusion. Here are three techniques to use when students read either digital or printed text.

- Think-Pair-Share, that old favorite, is easy to implement. Students partner up, and then after a given amount of time, the teacher directs the students to turn to their partner and discuss... (prompt provided by the teacher). The teacher may decide to have students share ideas with the entire group. Less able readers are going to hear how others are interpreting the text and will have more of a foundation when they go back and continue reading. (www.readingquest.org/strat/tps.html)

- The 30-15-5 plan works well as either a strategy to read for the big idea or a prelude to a second reading of the text with the purpose of answering questions that arose during the first read through (Wellman).

Figure 5-8. Activity

30-15-5: Read for the Big Idea

1. Divide the class into partners.
2. Provide an introduction to the text by setting both a context and purpose for reading.
3. Hand out the text and ask individuals to read. Alternatively, have partners read out loud to each other.
4. Explain that Partner A will talk about the text for 30 seconds and must talk the entire time. Comments might include:
   - Summarizing statements
   - Opinion statements about content
   - Questions
   - Connections to other text, the world, or self
   - Inferential statements
5. At the end of Partner A's time, Partner B speaks for 30 seconds, again speaking for the entire time. Partner B might respond to A's comments or use any of the topics mentioned above.
6. At the end of the second 30 seconds, the process repeats itself, except this time the time limit is 15 seconds for each person.
7. Ending the process is a third round that has a time limit of 5 seconds each.
8. Remind students that each person must speak about the text continuously during his or her turn.
9. Process the activity by asking for comments, summary statements, or questions to be pursued.

Note: this strategy could be used with text, video, read-alouds, etc., and times can be changed to be longer, such as 60-30-10.

- Just-Say-Something is a way to chunk text up in smaller sections that will ensure students won't get to the end totally confused.

Figure 5-9. Activity: Text Chunking

Just-Say-Something

1. Group students with a partner and designate one as A and the other B.
2. Working together, the pairs chunk up the reading by placing stop signs (stickies) along the way. Or, the teacher can decide ahead of time where students will stop.
3. Students read silently and stop at the stop signs. At the first stop, A "says something" about the text:
   - what she thinks it said
   - what she thinks about it
   - what interests her
   - what she has questions about
   - what new thoughts she has
   - what she might not have understood
   - how it connects with something else.
4. Then B responds. He may comment on something A said or make a comment of his own.
5. Partners resume reading and stop at the next stickie/stop sign. This time B gets to "say something" first, and then A responds.
6. Partners move on through the reading in this manner until they finish.

These strategies lend themselves to differentiation. You can pair students by reading readiness or interest, and you can use different texts on the same topic. By adding the conversation component, you address varied learning styles. Of critical importance to the activity is the teacher circulating and listening to the student conversations. By closely monitoring these activities, the teacher can quickly identify what students comprehend and where potential problems lurk. And remember, once one team teacher has taught the strategy, the other teachers can use it in their classes without having to teach the process. Teaming can be very efficient!

4 **Bonus —Visual literacy!** Today's world is a multimedia event. Images, sounds, and text bombard the senses. To effectively glean website information a student must integrate an understanding of the images with an understanding of the text. Teams, therefore, must incorporate strategies into their instruction that help students decipher the imagery of their multimedia world.

- The social studies teacher can initiate the process by using *Image Detective* (http://cct2.edc.org/PMA/image_detective/index.html). This site uses historical photographs to teach the viewer how investigators "read" a photo by using the inquiry method of posing a question, gathering and recording data by looking closely at the image, accessing prior knowledge, drawing some conclusions, and then by comparing the viewer's conclusion to those of others. This inquiry method is closely aligned to methodology used by scientists, so having the science classes repeat this process using images related to their studies reinforces both the scientific method and the skill of reading images. Language arts classes can reinforce these skills of interpretation by looking at provocative images designed to stimulate discussion and written expression. In math class, students can look at various images to find mathematical models lurking in nature.

- Another rich resource that will appeal to many teachers is at the National Archives site (www.archives.gov/education/lessons). This site provides study guides for students to analyze all sorts of media: cartoons, posters, maps, artifacts, motion pictures, as well as documents. One might be fooled into thinking that these activities are solely for the social studies/humanities classes. Wrong! These study guides are versatile enough to be used as is or adapted for a variety of purposes. When a teacher shares how she is using various guides, graphic organizers, and other strategies, teammates can build on those ideas and skills in their classrooms. Working together, team teachers can advance their students' critical thinking about the images that surround them.

- Young adolescents love comic books and are intrigued by *manga* (Japanese comics) and *anime* (Japanese-style animation). Take advantage of this interest to help students internalize concepts from any unit. Here's an activity that connects concepts from two or more subjects, helps students develop their understanding of plot development, and provides novelty to sustain their interest.

  - The language arts teacher and another subject teacher team up to design a project in which students demonstrate their understanding of a content concept (adaptation, racism, or patterns) by creating an original narrative in graphic novel or animation format.

  - Use the RAFT strategy to help students create their story line. RAFT stands for

    R = role of the writer
    A = audience for the piece
    F = format of the piece
    T = Task.

    In this strategy the teacher may assign all of the components, just one, or more. In the examples below, the students could choose their roles and the audience while the teacher designated the format (narrative graphic novel or animation) and the task (explaining a specific content concept). Here are two examples that might come from the same social studies/language arts collaboration in which racism across the centuries was the topic.

Figure 5-10. *RAFT example #1*

Creating a Story Line

- R = gladiator (student choice)
- A = Roman emperor (student choice)
- F = narrative/graphic novel (teacher choice)
- T = persuade the emperor that racism in the empire is a negative force (teacher/student negotiation).

Figure 5-11. RAFT example #2

Creating a StoryLine

- R = 1950s African-American rock and roll singer (student choice)
- A = his grandson (student choice)
- F = narrative/graphic novel (teacher choice)
- T = explain how the civil rights movement changed his personal and professional life (teacher/student negotiation)

The students have to create a narrative around the task. They must also include all of a narrative's components of character, conflict, setting, conflict resolution/climax, and denouement, plus they have the benefit of using images to bring the narrative vividly to life.

The reader is probably wondering about the need for students to have some artistic talent to create a graphic novel—a very good point. Here are some alternatives to make this task more doable.

- Pull in the art teacher to help students create their characters.

- Make a graphic novel one option among several. Having this option allows all artists to showcase their talents.

- Use an online animation tool like xtranormal (www.xtranormal.com) that creates the characters and automatically animates the script.

- Allow students to trace characters from other sources.

- Convince your school to purchase comic design software like Comic Life.

The reader may also be wondering if this is a rigorous assignment or just a fun task that allows students to play with paints (wet or digital). Nancy Frey and Douglas Fisher in *Teaching Visual Literacy* (2008) contend that the "stirring of the imagination" and critical thinking are end products of working with graphic novels (p. 34). Daniel Pink, author of *A Whole New Mind* (2009), argues that if we as a nation are to stay the predominant economic power, we have to be tremendous innovators. To do that we need our students looking at issues from many different perspectives including the visual arts. Combining text and imagery across curriculum boundaries in a task that asks students to recode an idea in a different genre and new format requires both critical and creative thinking—two attributes of rigor!

- Using images to teach metaphorical thinking is useful in every discipline. Metaphors help students think deeply and see shades of meaning. *Visual synectics* is a strategy that can be used over and over again, and yet is a different experience each time for the learner because the images and the topic change. When team teachers share this strategy, students develop the ability to understand metaphors. This strategy also differentiates because it allows the more advanced thinkers to make intuitive leaps and the more fragile learners to clarify their understanding by listening to others think out loud. Figure 5-12 explains how it works.

Figure 5-12.

Visual Synectics Activity

Process

- Students in groups of three form a circle.
- Individually they browse through the pictures that have been laid around the room. (The number of pictures should be at least double the number of participants.)
- Each student chooses a picture that "speaks" to him and returns to a chair in his small group circle.
- Students place pictures selected face down on the floor in front of them in the center of the circle of chairs.

When all are back in their circles:

- One student starts by describing how the image selected is like ... (The teacher may reveal a prompt that relates to the concept or topic being studied. How is your picture like events leading up to the Civil War? How is your picture like an ecosystem? How is your picture like polygons? How is your picture like the literary conflict in Tom Sawyer?)

- The student makes connections between the image with the topic.

- Still working with this same person and his image, the others in the group describe what they see and what connections they might make to that image (If that were my picture, I might notice or connect...).

- When everyone in the group has commented, person #1 gets the last word about the image.

- Repeat this process for each person in the group.

- If there is time, the group can discuss any patterns or overall connections that emerged from the conversations.

Uses

- In a single classroom visual synectics can be used as an assessment of prior knowledge, a summarizer, a method of formative assessment, and a review prior to an exam.

- Team teachers can use it in a whole team meeting as a way to build community, introduce a touchy subject such as bullying in a nonthreatening and engaging manner, or pique student interest in an upcoming integrated unit.

Visual literacy should not be relegated to second-class citizenship. It is a particularly important element in 21st century culture, and it enriches students' understanding of printed and digital text.

A last word from Jill...

Reading and writing are integral to the development of a student's cognitive abilities. People can no longer earn a living if they cannot read and write in print and digitally at sophisticated levels. Plus students who feel confident and competent in dealing with classroom materials are not apt to be discipline problems. Finally, students often do not do well on standardized tests because they cannot apply the behaviors of good readers to isolated text on a test and/or they lack sufficient background knowledge to fully comprehend the test item. Working together as a team to build student capacity for reading and writing benefits students in both the short and long run.

6

Close the Vocabulary Gap

The breadth of a student's vocabulary is a great indicator of their potential for academic success and their ability to comprehend all types of text. By working in concert, a middle grades team can increase student vocabulary prowess and thus increase student learning.

Attacking the Vocabulary Gap

"OK students, it's Free Rice Time! Eyes on the screen, and let's see how many grains of rice we can earn today toward our team goal of 1,000,000 grains of rice for the United Nations World Food Program!" (www.freerice.com).

"Here's our first word."

(On the screen):
baffle means:

> *a) perplex*
> *b) assess*
> *c) listen in*
> *d) treasure*

———————

So starts each Red Team homeroom twice a week. This ritual is a small step in the team's efforts to help students become global citizens and expand their vocabularies. Knowing that one encounter with a word in a vocabulary activity is useless, the four homeroom teachers choose a word each morning, and all four words are added to the team word wall. That's almost 300 new words a year just from this one brief activity. The word wall items are visited and revisited throughout the year so students have multiple encounters with these words. The Red Team teachers are always looking for ways to increase their students' mastery of vocabulary because they know a lack of vocabulary knowledge will impact student learning in each and every class.

Develop the depth and breadth of student vocabulary for three critical reasons:

- **The size of a student's written vocabulary is a sure-fire indicator of his or her potential academic success.**
  The relationship between vocabulary knowledge and academic achievement is well established. Robert Marzano (2004) states, "As early as 1941 researchers estimated that for students in grades 4 through 12, a 6,000-word gap separated students at the 25th and 50th percentiles on standardized tests" (p. 31). In our high-stakes testing environment, it makes sense for teachers to work together in addressing student needs that impact achievement in all content areas.

- **Reading comprehension in all content areas is affected by a student's breadth of Tier 2, or academic, vocabulary knowledge.**
  (Beck, McKeown, and Kucan, 2002). Students read in every subject. Sometimes it's an instruction manual, sometimes a novel, sometimes a webpage, or sometimes a newspaper or other print or digital informational text. Students may understand the content-specific vocabulary, but not the academic vocabulary words in the text. This deficiency keeps them from comprehending their assignments. It's imperative that teachers provide systematic instruction that increases students' abilities to comprehend sophisticated and complex text by increasing their depth of academic vocabulary knowledge.

- **People need 10-15 significant encounters with a new word to truly internalize it, according to Janet Allen.** It's nearly impossible for one teacher to provide all of those practices. Allen goes on to say, " The repetition that occurs incidentally during reading has to be made explicit when teaching critical words and concepts. It takes planning, flexibility, and variety to teach vocabulary in a way that students find pleasurable and challenging" (1999, p.35). She is referring to what a classroom teacher should do. Now imagine the potential for learning when students work with identified key words in different contexts across the curriculum. These numerous practices help the students build the multiple layers of understanding necessary to internalize new vocabulary.

Two Ways to Develop a Coordinated Approach to Building Student Vocabulary:

1 **As a team, choose three to five Tier 2 words each week to teach and reinforce.** Students lacking vocabulary knowledge will struggle with text because they do not understand the various contexts in which a word may be used and are therefore limited in their ability to comprehend text written above a fairly simplistic level. Traditional vocabulary instruction does not help students overcome this deficit, and thus they are still unable to comprehend text even when key content vocabulary has been pretaught. It's not just the technical words that cause confusion for low-achieving students, but also the lack of vocabulary depth.

There are three levels of vocabulary knowledge:

- **Tier 1** contains the most basic words (*table, pet, mother, run*).

- **Tier 2,** also known as academic vocabulary, contains "high-frequency words for mature language users" (Beck, 2007) such as *crucial, permeate,* and *critical*. Here are three characteristics of Tier 2 words that cause comprehension problems for students:

    - Tier 2 words are not often used in oral language or conversations, so students lack exposure to them.

    - Tier 2 words are often sophisticated synonyms for everyday concepts. Therefore, although students may be familiar with the concept, they do not recognize many synonyms. For example,

        > *Leery* or *wary* for the more commonly used *suspicious*

        > *Ravenous* for the more commonly used *very hungry*

    - Tier 2 words that are more apt to be found in writing than conversation. Students who grow up in homes without readily available reading material may not be familiar with these words.

- **Tier 3** contains words that are usually found in very specific types of text (content specific) and rarely in more general texts like fiction. These words are addressed in content classes within the context of the units in which they appear. For example, a math teacher teaches words such as *polygon, isosceles,* and *trapezoid* in a geometry unit. These words will seldom appear in language arts, music, or history classes.

Tier 2 words are the ones on which teams should focus their collaborative efforts. Here's a list of some Tier 2 words (www.academicvocabularyexercises.com/id21.htm).

adjacent	enormous	odd
albeit	forthcoming	ongoing
assemble	indicate	panel
collapse	integrity	persist
colleague	intrinsic	pose
compile	invoke	reluctance
conceive	levy	so-called
convince	likewise	straightforward

It's easy to assume that middle grade students know words such as these, but what if they don't? Think of the word *indicate* and its uses in a variety of contexts:

- *Indicate* the correct answer by circling it (any class).

- *Indicate* what materials you will need for your experiment in the right-hand column (science).

- Using examples from the text, *indicate* and substantiate what you think was the turning point in the Civil War (social studies).

- What are the *indicators* of a healthy life style? (health)

- When you go through the lunch line, *indicate* in a polite voice what your choice is for the main course.

- Don't forget to *indicate* on the registration form in which town you live.

If a student did not know the word *indicate*, she might be able to figure out the meaning from context clues. On the other hand, the student might just skip a direction or skim a piece of text briefly to avoid feeling frustrated by not knowing a key word and totally miss out on or misinterpret a piece of text.

Working collaboratively, team teachers can address the vocabulary gap that exists among their students by spending time each week on vocabulary development. In fact, it's simply wrong to ignore this issue because the middle grades are the last chance for students to develop the skills and habits that will help them be successful in high school and beyond. ACT's report, *The Forgotten Middle*, states that eighth grade achievement is the best predictor of whether or not a student will be ready for either a career or a post secondary education experience (2008). Students cannot achieve at high levels with a substandard vocabulary.

Each marking period identify which words the team will focus on by thinking about:

- Which content words are used in two or more classes (e.g., *variable, independence, value, tone, connections*)?

- Which Tier 2 words will the team teach? Peruse texts that you will be using across the curriculum and identify Tier 2 words that you anticipate might cause comprehension issues. A free online survey tool (Zoomerang or Survey Monkey) can be used to do preassessments of students' vocabulary knowledge.

- What are some really fun, sophisticated words to include that will challenge those students with a large vocabulary and interest those with a lesser knowledge of words—who will then love to show off using them (e.g., *arboreal, bulbous, interdigitation, unctuous, ignoramus*)?

Once the words are identified, create an instructional plan for each marking period that includes shared responsibility for direct instruction, multisensory multiple practices, and engaging instruction for students. Beck, McKeown, and Kucan, (2002) best describe effective vocabulary instruction, "A robust approach to vocabulary involves directly explaining the meanings of words along with thought-provoking, playful, and interactive follow-up" (p. 2). It makes sense for one team member to take responsibility each marking period to be the "keeper of the vocabulary flame." This team member will gently remind and push teammates not to forget their commitment to teach vocabulary even when other demands and responsibilities start to pile up.

Design a chart like the one below to keep track of the words the team chooses to work on together. Choose academic words that will be useful in multiple subjects such as *evidence*. Students need to show evidence when analyzing a character's' behavior, in writing up a science lab, or taking a stand in a debate for social studies. Also, notice that content-specific words can become the week's academic words. Though definitely a math word, *factors* has other meanings appropriate for use in other subjects, such as "These factors led to the extinction of this species," and "These factors made the conflict between the two characters even worse." By intentionally using words in multiple contexts, teachers help students become more sophisticated in their word use.

Figure 6-1. *Tracking chart for academic words*

1st Quarter	Academic Vocabulary	Language Arts	Science	Math	Social Studies
Week 1	indicate evidence conclusion	literary conflict	adapt adaptation	factors factoring	escarpment plateau butte
Week 2	factors adapt adjacent	rising action denouement	camouflage environment		summit continental divide
Week 3					
Week 4					
Week 5					
Week 6					
Week 7					
Week 8					

It's easy to keep a chart like this in a team notebook or on a team wiki. In addition to serving as a tracking tool, it also provides evidence that the team is working together to improve learning. At budget times when teams might face the chopping block because it appears to be cheaper not to maintain them, evidence like this chart help the leadership be persuasive when talking with central office personnel and school boards about the benefits of teams.

Teams will want to know whether their efforts are having any effect. Are students recognizing the words in their reading and using them in their writing? There are a couple of ways to gather evidence (there's that Tier 2 academic word again). In both cases, the team needs to know which words they want to concentrate on for the next month. Start slowly at the beginning of the year for teachers and students to feel comfortable and learn the system. Here are two ways to gather evidence of student vocabulary growth.

1. Use a graphic organizer such as Figure 6-2 that asks students to sort words according to their understanding of them. Hand out the sheet at the beginning of the month and then again at the end. See how many words have shifted from the *I don't have a clue* row to the *Hey! I've got it!* row. It's good feedback for the students because they have concrete evidence of their personal progress. (This is an adaptation of a Janet Allen strategy.)

2. Use one of the free online survey tools (Survey Monkey: www.surveymonkey.com or Zoomerang: www.zoomerang.com) to create an assessment. Have the students take the assessment several times during the year. The site automatically tallies the results so it is easy to track progress. Do not think of this assessment as a measure of individual students, but rather a formative assessment of how well the shared responsibility for vocabulary instruction is going. Keep it low key, and don't ask students to study. Share the results with students. "Look, everyone, in September 2% of the team knew what *intrinsic* means. Now in December, 47% know. Wow! Let's go for 100% by April." Discuss the results at team meeting to help assess what's effective and what's not, and then use the information to tweak the team's vocabulary instruction.

Figure 6-2. *Activity measuring vocabulary growth*

You may recognize some of the words below and not others. Write each word in the appropriate row below using the row titles as a guide		
assemble collapse colleague compile indicate integrity intrinsic invoke panel persist pose reluctance	I Don't Have A Clue What This Word Means!	
	I Have a Vague Idea What This Word Means, But I Wouldn't Want To Have to Explain It.	
	I've Got It! I Can Explain What This Word Means, and I Can Use It in Writing and Conversation	

2 **Agree on common graphic organizers for vocabulary that each teacher will use with research-based strategies.**

When students use a learning tool like a graphic organizer in a variety of classes, they become adept at using it. No longer do teachers need to use instructional time for explaining how to use the graphic organizer; rather, they can guide students in becoming better thinkers with the information gathered. Also, students often are reluctant learners because they prefer taking a zero to asking for help in front of their classmates when they do not understand how to do something. Seeing the use of a graphic organizer modeled by different teachers and completing the graphic organizers several times with peers is going to build students' confidence in their ability to independently use particular learning tools. Consider using the following four graphic organizers to help students internalize new words. Explicit directions are provided, or one can simply Google the name of the strategy to find examples.

Figure 6-3. Examples of graphic organizers

Graphic Organizer	Why It Works	When to Use It
Frayer Model	Describes the word Gives examples and non-examples (compares/contrasts) Students construct their own definitions. Images may be used.	Introducing the word Formative assessment Student practice
Linear Array	Shows relationship of word to others that are similar in nature. Provides a non-linguistic representation of the word's meaning.	Introducing the word Formative assessment Student practice Sponge activity at the beginning or end of class
Concept Circle	Connects word to other words with similar meanings or in the same category, or gives examples of the word. Provides a visual representation of the word.	Introducing the word Formative assessment Student practice Sponge activity at the beginning or end of class
Interactive Word Wall **Think of word walls as giant graphic organizers for the entire class to use together and individually.**	Provides a visual representation of words, especially when images are included. Facilitates multiple practices. Provides scaffolding for ELL learners and students with expressive language difficulties. Shows relationship of words to one another	Introduction of the word Student practice Wall sized thesaurus when students are writing and speaking Sponge activity at the beginning or end of class

Let's look at each type of graphic organizer in the table above. The **Frayer Model** is a graphic organizer that examines words from different perspectives.

Figure 6-4. *Template for Frayer Model*

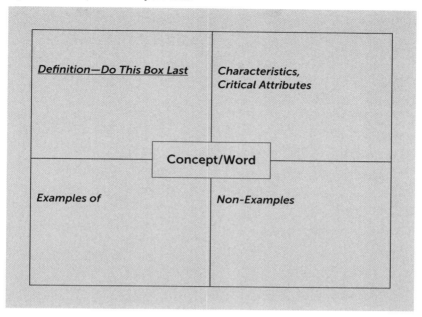

When teaching a word for the first time, the teacher posts a blank Frayer model on a large chart or overhead transparency or uses an LCD projector with a computer. Sometimes paper or transparencies are easier to manipulate and write on than using a computer, but that is a matter of personal choice. Then the teacher uses the following steps to describe the word:

1. Write the word/concept in the center box.

2. List the characteristics or critical attributes that describe the word or concept. See Figure 6-5 for an example on satire.

3. List concrete examples of the word that students can relate to their experiences. Sometimes people confuse characteristics and examples. Examples are objects, processes, or people that exist in reality or media. Characteristics are descriptors.

4. List non-examples, again using items that students can relate to their own experiences.

5. Write a definition that makes use of the characteristics and examples. DO NOT just copy a textbook or dictionary definition. You are modeling the construction of a definition in your own words.

Figure 6-5. Example #1 of Frayer Model

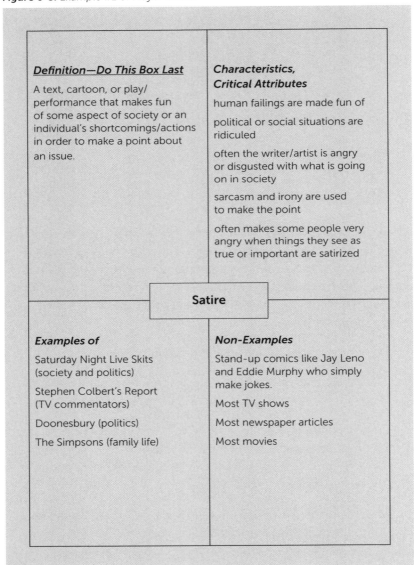

Sometimes the best way to teach a process is with a topic from real life that students can relate to. Here's an example using chocolate.

Figure 6-6. *Example #2 of Frayer Model*

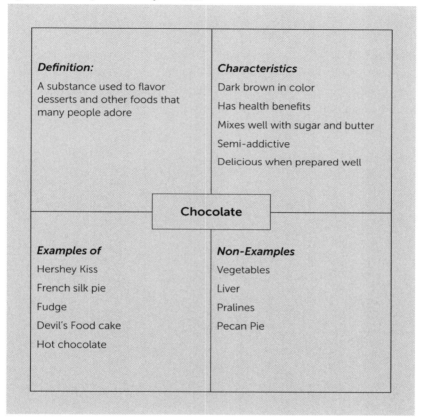

Linear Arrays (Allen, 1999) show how a word is related to other words. All of the words in the array are connected to a topic or concept. The array also demonstrates degree along a continuum. For example, consider the topic of personal spending habits. The opposite ends of the continuum might be *miser* and *conspicuous consumer*. Words in between might be *spendthrift, skinflint, saver, spender,* and *penny-pincher*. By using a linear array similar to the one below to teach the words, teachers help students build a mental map of the degrees of personal finance.

miser...skinflint...penny-pincher...saver...spender...spendthrift...
conspicuous consumer

An example from geography might help students grasp different geographic land features—from flat land to the top of a plateau.

valley floor ... plain ... escarpment...plateau

Concept Circles (Vacca and Vacca, 1989) can be used in a variety of ways to introduce a word/concept. They can be used to demonstrate examples or show synonyms. Here's an example of a concept circle for the word *dictator* that uses examples.

Figure 6-7. Example #1 Concept Circle

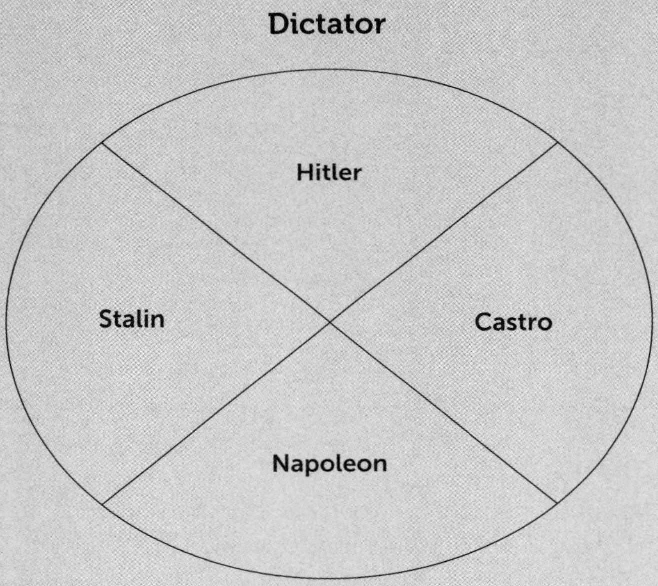

A **dictator** is a person who totally controls a country. The circle contains 4 examples of historic dictators.

Another concept circle might list the characteristics of the word or concept. Here's one for *amphibian*.

Figure 6-8. *Example #2 Concept Circle*

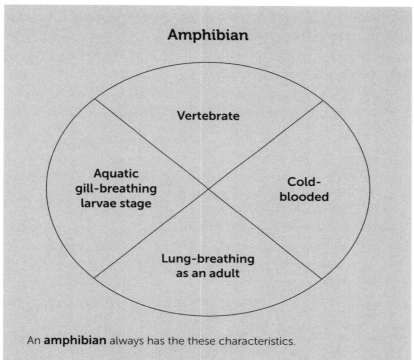

An **amphibian** always has the these characteristics.

Adding images to the concept circles will help students create mental images of the word and its characteristics. Students can also add additional details. For example, with the dictator example, the teacher might divide the class into four groups, one for each dictator. The teacher then would give the groups ten minutes to conduct Internet searches to find collaborating details that align with the characteristics that the teacher has already given. This additional work would continue to build students' understanding of the concept. Concept circles can also be used to check for understanding. The teacher leaves part of the circle blank, and the students fill in the missing parts.

Agreeing to use a common graphic organizer to teach new vocabulary is a simple, no-risk first step for a team to take that will benefit their students. However, to avoid having the work become monotonous through use of the same graphic organizer across the team too often, teachers and students should devise novel ways to use the graphic organizers such as making foldables or turning the graphic organizer into a kinesthetic experience.

Figure 6-9. *Foldable Frayer Model Directions*

To make a foldable version of Frayer Model.

- Place an 8 1/2 X 11 piece of paper flat on the table with the 11" side at the top.
- Fold the both sides (left and right) in toward the center. Edges should meet but not overlap—looks a bit like a shutter. Crease well.
- Fold in half — top to bottom
- Open up and cut each "shutter" in half. Start cuts on single edges. You should now have four flaps attached to a large square area.

- Label the four flaps; Definition, Characteristics, Examples of, Non-Examples. Write the word/concept on the center of the flaps.
- Under each flap students write the appropriate information and on the large flat area they should draw a representation of the word or concept.

  (Adapted from Dinah Zike's *Reading and Study Skills Foldables*)

Interactive Word Walls.

Once thought of as an elementary school strategy, word walls are now used nationally by middle and high school teachers across the content areas with great success. Easily set up, word walls require chart paper, markers, and a bit of wall space to post the charts. Word walls should be created in each team member's room using the following steps.

- Choose three to five Tier 2, or academic words, in addition to key content words to emphasize each week in every class.

  - List them on a chart, and make sure students can read them from anywhere in the room.

  - Include key concept words from other team members' word walls, and use them as part of your ongoing review and practice.

  - Use online podcasts to teach new words. A variety of podcasts are free on the Web. One, the Princeton Review Vocab Minute found at the site listed below, is set to music and done with humor. Podcasts provide variety in instruction—a different voice than the teacher's. They also are a great resource for differentiation. Linguistically gifted students often love words and word study; connect them to one of the free-subscription podcasts, and you have a self-paced vocabulary program that offers challenging words. A variety of podcasts can be found at www.learnoutloud.com/PodcastDirectory/Languages/Vocabulary-Building.

  - Explore www.webcorp.org.uk/wcadvanced.html to find sentences on the Web using key words. Paste text into www.nottingham.ac.uk/~alzsh3/acvocab/awlhighlighter.htm. The site automatically highlights the academic words contained in the text.

- Make a point to use them in your teaching.

  - Encourage students to refer to them when writing and speaking, perhaps giving bonus points for their usage.

  - Play games with them.

  - Point to them when teaching.

- Use them as a sponge activity (see below).

- Use them to review and summarize information.

- Hold contests during homeroom or advisory, give awards for the best sentence using all five words of the week, write raps, poems, etc.

- Create podcasts that students can download to their favorite media player. A podcast allows students to hear the correct pronunciation of the word, the definition explained in kid-friendly language with examples relevant to their lives, and the words used in multiple sentences. Having a podcast available 24/7 allows students to go back and review the word as many times as they need to without worrying about their friends thinking they are stupid. Teachers and/or students can create podcasts using Garage Band on Macs and with Audacity, a download app for PCs.

- With students create visuals that show the words used correctly in different contexts.

- Use word walls as a modification for students with speech and language retrieval issues. These students have brain-processing issues that keep them from retrieving words on demand. If the purpose of the assessment is to check whether a student understands a concept, then there should not be any problem with students having a word bank as a prompt (either allowing everyone access to the word wall or providing specified students with index cards with the list of words on them). Retrieval and understanding are two different learning objectives.

- Employ them to help second language learners who need to hear and see these words more often than native speakers. Point to the word each time it is used in class to reinforce the pronunciation, the spelling, and the meaning of the word. Attaching images to the words is also helpful. Actually, these actions will help all students.

Some might wonder, "Why not use wikis or another digital tool for the word walls?" Putting the words online so that students have 24/7 access is a good strategy, however, it does not replace a highly visible word wall in the classroom. When words are posted on a wall, they are easily accessible for the teacher and students to incorporate them minute-to-minute in the lesson. An individual can simply walk to the wall and point to a particular word. It's quick, provides an instant visual prompt, and doesn't take time away from the lesson. Teams will find benefits in using both physical and digital versions of the word wall.

Make word walls interactive. Below is a list of very quick ways to provide nonthreatening practices for students to learn how to use words correctly. They only take a few minutes to do, so each of the team members ought to be able to fit in such a review once or twice a week, thus providing students with multiple encounters with important vocabulary words.

- **Everyone up:** *Raise your hand and when I call on you, tell me the definition of one of these words, and then you can sit down.* Word of caution! Don't get into a staring contest with a student who hasn't raised his hand—keep things positive. Just look at the wall clock and say, *Oh, we're out of time, everyone still standing, please sit down. Sorry I didn't get to everyone this time.*

- **First one out the door:** *Raise your hand and use one of our words in a sentence, and you can be the first one in line to leave for lunch!*

- **Review and summarize** information:

  > *Please tell us how photosynthesis and respiration are related.*

  > *Please compare and contrast photosynthesis and respiration.*

  > Note: Put names on popsicle sticks and keep them in a can. Pull them out randomly to keep students on their toes. Whatever you do, don't call a student's name before you ask the question because then everyone else stops listening and thinking!

- **Use pop culture** to provide students practice with words in different contexts. For example, think of the words—evasive, pinnacle, and prevaricate.

    Name a character in a video or online game who could be described as evasive.

    Name some characters on TV who are at the pinnacle of their careers.

    Think of a character in movie who prevaricates.

- **Use sentence stems** that require students to demonstrate their understanding of a word by finishing the sentence:

    The stairs to the building were dilapidated so....

    My little brother has an uncanny way of...

- **Create a scenario** by connecting vocabulary words in sentence or question and have students respond:

    Would a contemporary of George Washington consider allowing women to vote a radical idea?

    Would you be forthcoming if you were in the process of dissembling to your parents?

Note: many of the above ideas come from Isabel Beck (2007).

Next Steps

Provide multiple short, multisensory, nonthreatening practices. When teachers collaborate, the opportunities for providing multiple practices with words explode. Think of the possibilities:

- Sponge activities
- Ticket Out the Door activities
- Formative assessments
- Homeroom competitions

Moving through three or four classes a day, a student has several opportunities to see, hear, and practice using new words in fun and interesting ways during a typical school week. Several such opportunities are described below.

1 **Sponge activities are designed to soak up extra class minutes that are often wasted at the beginning or end of a class.** Engaging sponge activities can energize students and prepare them for the upcoming class. At the end of the class, they ensure that students are leaving with a final review of an important idea or concept. Include Tier 2 words and other content-specific words as well as your own. Some examples include:

- Play Hangman with new words for five minutes; to solve the puzzle students also need to explain what the word means.

- Utilize popular comics and cartoons; put on the screen a cartoon or comic without a caption or word bubble and ask students to write a quip or two using new words.

- Mix and match: write words on one color of index card and definitions on index cards of another color. Distribute them to students with instructions to find the student that holds the matching definition or word. Turn on a jazzy tune to create an energized ambiance as they mill about in search of their partners.

2 **Tickets Out the Door or Exit Cards** are used during the last five minutes of class to help students internalize ideas and concepts. They also serve as a formative assessment to inform the teacher about the level of understanding on the part of the students. A Ticket Out the Door gives the teacher information on what to review the next day in class. Teachers can support one another by using each other's content words. Suppose the science teacher is not sure if students understand some content vocabulary and wants to check in a nonthreatening manner the level of student mastery. She could ask each of her teammates to use different words in an Exit Card and collect them at the end of the day. She can get a read on three times as many words as if she just used this strategy herself. This week the science teacher receives some help, and next week it's the social studies or math teacher who requests some assistance. Tickets Out the Door are fast and easy and provide timely feedback on student understanding of key vocabulary.

Figure 6-10. *Examples of questions for Tickets Out the Door*

3-2-1 Activity

1. Write
   - **3** words you know so well you could teach tomorrow (Be prepared!)
   - **2** synonyms for...
   - **1** word you do not understand.
2. Use this word correctly in a sentence.
3. Draw a picture that illustrates the meaning of this word.

3 **Formative Assessments** that are embedded in classroom instruction help the teacher and learner identify critical evidence of learning as the students strive to meet a well-articulated goal (Black and Wiliam). Both the student and teacher use this evidence to shape their next steps in the learning process. Checking for comprehension of vocabulary gives both the teacher and students feedback on the level of understanding of key concepts. Effective formative assessments can be very simple in format.

- **One-sentence summaries:** *Everyone grab a marker and write a one-sentence summary of this concept.* Two minutes later have students hold their papers up over their heads so everyone can see. The teacher gets a quick view of level of understanding, and all students see the main point restated in a variety of ways. You can use rolls of cash register tape, and easily snip off strips for students to use for sentences. Here is an example of a one-sentence summary of "factors."

  Factors are the numbers we multiply to get another.

- Use the **Frayer Model** as an assessment. Group students, give them chart paper, and assign them a couple of words to review using the Frayer Model. The charts are easily shared and checked by the teacher.

- **Concept Circles** can also be used as formative assessments. By leaving one or more sections blank in the circle, teachers are able to ascertain students' levels of understanding of a word by quickly scanning answers.

4 **Competitions** can be engaging and fun ways to get students to practice using new words. They shouldn't be used every day, but using them regularly in a lighthearted manner will show the students that exploring words can be fun as well as a way for them to boost their communication skills. Here are just a few ideas.

- Homeroom Jeopardy, Password, So You Want to Be a Millionaire

- Limericks, song lyrics, raps to be shared or published (Class/ team blogs, wikis, webpages, etc.)

- Scrabble and other word games (online versions exist)

- Get the principal, cafeteria staff, and other school staff involved by giving them a list of words for the week and asking them to stop your students whenever they see them. Your "helpers" can ask students to define the words or use them correctly in a sentence. If the student can do this, he receives a ticket that goes into a jar in each homeroom. Recognition can be given for the homeroom with the most tickets or the team can hold drawings for prizes.

- Google "Word Games" and a host of free online resources pops up. Be sure to check them out before sending the students to them.

5 **Creative visual representations using free Web 2.0 tools**

- xtranormal (www.xtranormal.com). Using text they write, students can create online animation movies.

- Blabber (http://blabberize.com). Students use their own images and voice to create a short animated movie.

- Glogster(http://edu.glogster.com). Students create posters online. There is a site just for educators to provide protection from unsuitable material.

- Animoto (http://animoto.com). Students can demonstrate their understanding of words and concepts through images and music.

6 **Three more engaging ways to provide practice with new words.** These techniques can be easily incorporated into individual classes or used as a whole team activity.

- Creating a **visual representation** of vocabulary words is a key step for students as they internalize these new words. Researchers report that recoding or representing information in non-linguistic formats increases achievement (Marzano, Sprenger). Here is a strategy that combines visual representation and cooperative work.

   Process:
   - Divide students into partners or groups of three.
   - Hand out chart paper and markers.

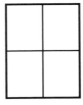

   - Have students fold paper into fourths.
   - Give each group four words to express visually.

- Direct students to create a visual representation for each of their four words.
- Have students share their work with the rest of the class.

Some teachers use names developed by Dina Zike (www.dinah.com/manipulatives.php) for her foldable manipulatives when giving directions. A fold along the horizontal axis is called a hamburger fold and a fold along the vertical axis is called a hot dog fold. If a team chooses to use these names or others that they devise, once the students know them, directions can be more easily given and executed.

- **Showing relationships** among unit words is also an important step in vocabulary instruction (Kuzmich). Some words are Big Ideas and others are supporting details. Think about teaching about the United States' form of government. Executive branch, legislative branch, judicial branch, and federalism are all key big ideas that have a lot of vocabulary associated with them. It's important that students see the relationship among the words. Graphic organizers help with this process. Students can create word webs by hand, however, there is a terrific, free Web-based tool that allows students or teachers to demonstrate the relationship among words. It is Bubbl.us (http://bubbl.us). Here is a web made at Bubbl.us.

Figure 6-11. Example of web showing relationships among words.

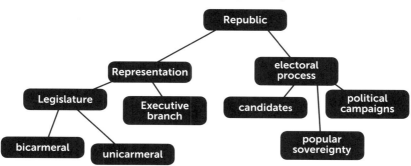

In this case, the key word is republic and the web shows how the other new vocabulary words are related to it. Helping students visualize how words are related helps them develop a keener, deeper understanding of new terms.

- **Cue cards** can be a way of encouraging students to use new words in a correct context while contributing to class discussion. It's a very simple process and one in which teachers can help each other out. As students enter the classroom, give each one an index card with a vocabulary word on it. The words might come from the current unit under study, from another teacher's content list of words, or from the list of academic words the entire team is working on. Encourage the students to use the word in class discussions or while asking a question. To help students who might be unsure of their word, give the class three minutes of time to use any resource in the room, including people, to clarify the meaning. Students will get into this strategy and think of all sorts of original ways to insert their words into what's going on. When a word is used incorrectly, gently give some hints so the student can reuse the word correctly. Have fun with this strategy.

It's important that a team knows to which strategies students have been introduced so that they may be used regularly. Each team has to figure out how to facilitate that communication. They might keep the information in a team notebook, wiki, or on a form. An easy way is to create a 5 x 8 index card for each strategy the team chooses to use. Flip though those index cards regularly at a team meeting, and take a minute to note who has introduced or used which strategy in the last two weeks. Once a quarter spread all the cards out on a table, and view them together. Make a notation on the strategies that are working well and how they have been adapted; have a conversation about trying new ones. The team has a record of collaboration and reflection. This record will be helpful in discussing with the administration the team's work and for planning the next year's work. This entire process could also be digitized.

Vocabulary development is a critical piece of the learning puzzle. It must be a shared responsibility across content areas if students are going to be able to read a variety of print and digital texts with meaning and communicate their ideas effectively. When teams take the time to coordinate their approach to vocabulary instruction, reinforce each other's key content terms, and engage students in creative and enjoyable word study, they send a message to their students that an excellent spoken and written vocabulary is valued and integral to student success.

A last word from Jill...

Please, please, please do not ask students to look up words in the dictionary and then use them in a sentence. This old practice is simply not effective for several reasons.

- Students quite likely won't know which definition applies to the context they need to use. For example look at the possibilities for a simple word like fresh:

    1. newly made or obtained: fresh footprints.

    2. recently arrived; just come: fresh from school.

    3. new; not previously known, met with, etc.; novel: to uncover fresh facts; to seek fresh experiences.

    4. additional or further: fresh supplies.

    5. not salty, as water.

    6. retaining the original properties unimpaired; not stale or spoiled: Is the milk still fresh?

7. not preserved by freezing, canning, pickling, salting, drying, etc.: fresh vegetables.

8. not tired or fatigued; brisk; vigorous: She was still fresh after that long walk.

9. not faded, worn, obliterated, etc.: fresh paint; a fresh appearance.

10. looking youthful and healthy: a fresh beauty that we all admired.

11. pure, cool, or refreshing, as air.

12. denoting a young wine, esp. a white or rosé, that is clean, crisp, and uncomplicated.

13. Meteorology. (of wind) moderately strong or brisk.

14. inexperienced; green; callow: Two hundred fresh recruits arrived at the training camp.

15. Informal. forward or presumptuous.

16. (of a cow) having recently given birth to a calf.

17. Slang: (a) exciting; appealing; great.(b).informed; up-to-date.—noun

18. the fresh part or time.

19. a freshet.—verb (used with object), verb (used without object)

20. to make or become fresh.—adverb

21. newly; recently; just now: He is fresh out of ideas. The eggs are fresh laid.

Imagine the confusion that exists when students are looking up a totally unfamiliar word!

- Writing a new word in a sentence is ineffective because students do not have enough practice with new words to use them in meaningful ways. Students need multiple guided and nonthreatening (ungraded) practices using and hearing others use the words in multiple contexts before being assessed on their ability to use the word properly in a specified context.

- Writing the words multiple times is boring! Copying words bores students to tears, and vocabulary study becomes drudgery rather than interesting and fun. Although it may help some students learn to spell the word, this activity provides absolutely no practice in correct usage. It is just a "no-no."

Some readers may be thinking, "How in the world can I add all these vocabulary activities to my classes when my content requirements are all ready bubbling over the top? I just don't have time!" Sure, time is an issue for everyone so finding ways to work together will help to alleviate this pressure. When both interdisciplinary teams and exploratory teams collaborate by infusing academic and content words into the everyday fabric of their classes, students' learning in all classes will improve. Success in all educational activities depends on having a good vocabulary: vocabulary instruction simply cannot be ignored.

7

Embrace the
Digital Revolution!

Our students are digital natives having lived with the Internet, cell phones, and computers all their lives. Some of their teachers, on the other hand, remember a world without even TV, and many reached adulthood before computers were common. Therefore, teams must work together to understand and capitalize on the learning possibilities these still-foreign-to-many-adults digital tools provide.

The Arrival

The team gazed at the stacks and stacks of gleaming white laptops. There were almost 100 of the machines, one for each student and teacher. Power cords were also in piles. One hundred of those, too, one for each machine. The inventory list also mentioned "dongles." What are they? The team just stood in awe of their new teaching tool, not quite sure of what to do next.

"I'm excited, let's get started. Let's pass them out tomorrow! I can't wait to use them in my social studies class—we can visit all of the ancient sites mentioned in the textbook. Every student can be exploring a different site. Here, I'll take this stack into my room," said Freddie as she started to grab some laptops.

"Whoa! Hold up! We have to think about some things," declared Lisa. "Things like storage, checking them out in the morning and in at the end of school, charging them, not to mention teaching the students how to use them."

"That's right. What's the rush? Let's just get school started, and then maybe in October or November we can tackle distribution of these things," added Jason. "I don't see what the big hurry is. I don't anticipate using them very often."

Freddie could hardly contain her enthusiasm, "The big deal is that these laptops will change how students learn forever! I have a friend whose students e-mail and video chat with experts on ecosystems all over the world. Her students are learning firsthand about our planet's fragility. Another friend uses the record function all of the time for *students who have language difficulties. I know I jump into things too quickly, and Lisa is right—we need to have a plan, but..."*

Carlos, the team's detail person, put up chart paper, and the team began to brainstorm all of the issues surrounding the deployment and use of the new laptops. They knew from experience that things went more smoothly when they worked together to anticipate issues and were proactive in designing solutions beforehand. Although they didn't all share the same level of enthusiasm for the devices, they would work together to ensure that implementation went smoothly.

One-to-one computing, that is, each student having his or her own device, is growing in schools, and this trend will continue. The devices may be different—full fledged laptops, handhelds like iTouches or Palm Pilots, or digital notebooks, iPads, or something that's not even on the market yet—but they will be available to all. When students have access to these devices, teaching and learning changes. Digital learning has many of the same issues as more traditional approaches: instructional practices, classroom management, the ethics of intellectual property, quality of resources, and care of the equipment, among others. There are also new things to consider—additional skills that need to be included in the curriculum, digital citizenship, and safety. While some educators embrace the digital opportunities and challenges, others are reluctant or even fearful. A team that works collaboratively to define and implement policies and procedures and shares strategies for integrating digital learning will make the most of these technological marvels.

Embrace digital learning and integrate it into your pedagogical practice because...

- **Digital devices offer teachers ways to address student learning differences that no other generation could imagine!**

    - Visual learners can watch interactive simulations as many times as they need to in order to understand and master new knowledge.

- Teachers can use Jing (www.jingproject.com) and other digital tools to create visuals of procedures that students can refer to for support. Digital tools allow teachers to scaffold new learning in a multitude of ways.

- Students with expressive and receptive language issues can use the speech and record tools on their computers to further their learning. A free app for smart phones, Dragon Dictation, allows people to dictate into their phones and turns the dictations into text. The dictation can then be e-mailed to a computer, where it can be downloaded to become the first draft of an essay.

- Teachers can easily differentiate through reading readiness, interest, and cognitive development because the Web resources on any given topic are so rich.

- Students can demonstrate new learning in a myriad of ways—podcasts, movies, slide shows, essays, PowerPoints, and animations.

- Students can create new knowledge, share it with the world, and receive feedback.

- Students with organizational issues will have their work all in one place when they are assigned a device of their own. Work doesn't get lost in a locker or disappear into the bottomless backpack. One of the major irritants between teacher and student—lost work—virtually disappears.

- Students with sight and hearing impairments have access to assistive technology that allows them to participate more easily in the regular classroom.

- **Creativity and innovation drive economic growth in this century, and schools play a major role in developing these attributes in a community's citizens.** Computers and digital tools provide "fertile soil" for developing these critical abilities that our country needs to stay a vital, dynamic democracy. Read and reflect on these statements of Stephen Heppell, one of Europe's leading experts on online learning.

Computers are everyday tools for us all, seen or unseen, but their value in learning is as tools for creativity and learning rather than as machines to "deliver" the curriculum. These tools, in our children's hands, are forever pushing the envelope of expertise that previous technologies excluded them from: they compose, quantize and perform music before acquiring any ability to play an instrument, they shoot, edit and stream digital video before any support from media courses, they produce architectural fly-throughs of incredible buildings without any drafting or 2D skills, they make stop frame animations with their Plasticine models, they edit and finesse their poetry, they explore surfaces on their visual calculators, swap ideas with scientists on-line about volcanic activity, follow webcam images of Ospreys hatching, track weather by live satellite images, control the robots they have built and generally push rapidly at the boundaries of what might be possible, indeed what was formerly possible, at any age (Heppell, www.heppell.net/weblog/stephen).

Heppell describes learning experiences that some children now enjoy. These scenarios are still far from the norm in almost any middle school, but eventually they will be common practice. When we ignore these digital tools that students use at home, we risk students becoming even less engaged in learning at school and waste opportunities to help all students develop their creativity and innovative thinking skills. Digital learning experiences in the classroom provide the authenticity of real world problem solving never before available.

- **Long talked about instructional and curriculum reforms come to fruition with one-to-one computing.** Educators from all over the world visit Maine to learn about successfully implementing a one-to-one program as the Maine Learning Technology Initiative has done for the last 8 years. Every seventh and eighth grade student and teacher in the state has a laptop. One of the observations invariably made by visitors is that the teachers are out in the classroom coaching individuals or groups of students rather than standing at the front of the room delivering a steady flow of information. They also like the student collaboration, problem solving, and creativity they see. These characteristics are the ones they want developed in their classrooms back home, and they quickly become convinced that one-to-one devices are the catalysts that will indeed bring about the pedagogical shift called for by the middle school movement during the past 20-30 years.

- **Middle grades classrooms that fail to provide students with 21st century learning tools that push beyond classroom walls to explore, collaborate, and create will be obsolete.** Online learning opportunities have grown exponentially in the past decade. Teachers are no longer the only experts students can turn to for knowledge. Information is everywhere. Young adolescents themselves can now find information on all the state standards. They can also locate tutors and virtual communities of learners on the Web. Even face-to-face interaction is available through Skype and other communication tools. Below are quoted findings from a study sponsored by the John D. and Catherine MacArthur Foundation (www.macfound.org):

  - Youth are navigating complex social and technical worlds by participating online.

    - Young people are learning basic social and technical skills that they need to fully participate in contemporary society.

    - The social worlds that youth are negotiating have new kinds of dynamics, as online socializing is permanent, public, involves managing elaborate networks of friends and acquaintances, and is always on.

  - Young people are motivated to learn from their peers online.

    - The Internet provides new kinds of public spaces for youth to interact and receive feedback from one another.

    - Young people respect each other's authority online and are more motivated to learn from each other than from adults.

  - Most youth are not taking full advantage of the learning opportunities of the Internet.

- Most youth use the Internet socially, but other learning opportunities exist.

- Youth can connect with people in different locations and of different ages who share their interests, making it possible to pursue interests that might not be popular or valued with their local peer groups.

- "Geeked-out" learning opportunities are abundant—subjects like astronomy, creative writing, and foreign languages.

On the surface it might appear that the role of the school will be diminished, however, middle grades teachers recognize that the saying "The whole is greater than the sum of it parts" applies to their teams. The synergy generated when concerned adults work together to address the cognitive, social, psychological, and physical needs of young adolescents cannot be duplicated on the Web. Using research like the MacArthur Foundation study on how adolescents use Web resources will help the team think strategically about their curriculum and instruction in a one-to-one world. However, if teachers choose to teach as if it were still the late 1900s, they will become irrelevant to their students despite their good intentions. Effective team dynamics plus digital learning opportunities make an unbeatable combination.

- **Wise use and safety issues must be addressed.** The school is the community's prime vehicle for educating students, parents, and others about critical issues. Fire prevention week always has a school component; many families recycle because of a child's participation in a unit focusing on reducing, reusing, and recycling; and recent fears about flu epidemics were addressed with school inoculations and closings. The schools now have an obligation to educate their students and parents about using the Internet safely and wisely and to correct the misinformation circulating through the mass media and the Web about this issue. A middle grades team that has established solid relationships with its students and parents is in the perfect position to help their students and families understand the wonderful potential of the Web as well as how to be intelligent and safe consumers of its information.

Steps to Take

1 **Take charge of your team's own professional development.**
Too often new technological devices are deployed with little professional development and problems quickly arise. When this occurs, people tend to pull the devices out of the classroom, but no team wants to lose access to these marvelous teaching-learning tools.

- As a team visit a school that is integrating technology throughout its programs. Go with a list of things to find out. How has it changed their instruction? What have been their challenges? How do they organize things? Talk with students to find out how they feel about their devices. Are they just being used as digital worksheets or is something more substantive going on? Chances are the team will arrive back at school with more questions than answers. But firsthand experiences have a way of helping people formulate a vision of what might be.

- Visit schools virtually by way of their websites. Websites often have policies and procedures listed, examples of student work, and contact information so further research can be conducted through e-mail. Here are two sites to explore:

  > Skowhegan Area Middle School (Maine): www.msad54.k12.me.us/sams
  > Click on any of these links to learn more about technology integration at this school: Library/Media, Technology Integration, Special Student Projects, History Podcasts, Skowhegan Community Project.

  > Lilla G. Frederick Pilot Middle School (Boston): www.lgfnet.org
  > Look at the Technology section of their menu. There are resources on expectations, rules, and what a typical day looks like for a student with a laptop.

- Secure a copy of John Palfry and Urs Gasser's *Born Digital: Understanding the First Generation of Digital Natives* (2008), and as a team read Chapter 4 on safety. This chapter discusses the big topics of Internet safety: pornography and cyber bullying. It is a nonhysterical look at these two issues, and the authors put these issues in the context of society as whole, not just its technological side. This information will give the team a good foundation in understanding safety issues and help them construct their role in keeping students safe. The entire book is very much worth reading, and once you start it, you will inevitably be drawn into all its resources.

- Become familiar with Web resources that provide reliable information on Internet issues and digital learning. Here are two: the John D. and Catherine MacArthur Foundation has a page on Digital Media and Learning: Google MacArthur + Digital Media and Learning and Pew Internet and American Life Project: www.pewinternet.org/Topics.aspx

- Read several technology blogs. The bloggers may be writing about tools not available in your school, however reading the commentaries provides insight as to trends and what is happening around the world—great information for teachers to have in mind. To get started check out David Warlick's blog at http://davidwarlick.com/2cents. He is an author, consultant, and educator who stays current with happenings in the digital world.

2 **Develop team procedures for organizing, storing, maintaining, and using the devices.** Laptops or hand-helds cannot just be shoved into lockers or piled up on a bookcase or table. There has to be a plan. Sometimes schools provide charging carts and sometimes they don't. Plastic crates with dividers designed for folders often work well as substitute storage units. Laptops fit into them, and there is space for the charging cord to snake out and connect with a power strip. Most devices won't hold their charge for an entire day, so the team has to figure out how to recharge. Having power cords all over the room during classes creates a tripping hazard. Some schools address this issue by having the students return to homeroom to plug in during lunch, so the device will last through the afternoon. Other schools set up a battery charging station in a central location, and when the battery runs out, the students go there and exchange batteries. Whatever the procedure, the team must make sure that the students get into the routine quickly and smoothly. Practice does make perfect. Each device has its own needs, so it is impossible to have a thorough "to-do" list here.

Also critical is for the team to discuss how they will handle students who misuse the machines. The knee-jerk reaction is to take away the device as a punishment. The team has to ask itself a couple of questions—if a student wrote a note in class, would they take away his pencil? If a student hid an inappropriate magazine in a textbook, would they take away the textbook? The answer of course is, "No." The pencil and the textbook are tools for learning as is the computer or other hand-held device. Taking it away is limiting the student's ability to access the curriculum; so other consequences need to be in place. There is no easy answer to this dilemma. However, by taking the time to anticipate the procedures and policies that need to be in place and to devise a plan ahead of time, deployment and implementation of a one-to-one digital learning program will go more smoothly.

3   **Rethink the room arrangement.** The traditional room setup with the teacher up front peering out over rows of desks that all face forward is a recipe for off-task behavior. Although digital learning engages the students, kids will be kids, and they sometimes venture off the assigned task. And...they are quick! By the time a teacher makes it from the front of the room to the back, they have visited five music and video sites and are back on task looking innocent. It doesn't do any good to get upset. Smile and then think of better ways to arrange the room to cut down on off-task behavior. Small groups or a U-shape arrangement of desks makes it much easier for the teacher to make a visual sweep of the room to see student screens. Some teachers prefer the flying wedge—rows of desks slanted in a V shape—and others prefer a giant X. Team teachers should experiment to find the best arrangement for their rooms. The best defense—and offense—is always being on the move, monitoring and coaching students as they work within a furniture arrangement that facilitates such actions.

4   **Pre-assess to find out exactly what your students know about various devices, the Web, and searching.** Do not assume that students are experts just because they've been around computers all of their lives. They know a lot, but not everything. For example, many people may not know that turning off the airport when not using the Internet may conserve power and help the charge last longer. Or, unless students have had previous teachers who taught them to evaluate the quality of websites, they are probably not skilled at this process (see the next chapter). The team needs to know what skills need to be explicitly taught, which ones need to be reinforced, and which have already been mastered.

5 **Add time and task management to your study skills program.** The word "multitasking" is bandied around to the point that many people accept it as a fact of life. Folks of all ages claim they are capable of listening to music, responding to e-mail, conversing via Instant Messaging, and doing serious work all at the same time. However, that concept might be more accurately named "serial tasking." Marilee Sprenger addresses this myth in "Focusing the Digital Brain" in *Educational Leadership* (2009). She credits software executive Linda Stone with creating the phrase *continuous partial attention* to describe the process of attempting to address several tasks at once. Furthermore, a study at Stanford University reports that people who try to multitask are outperformed on tasks every time by those who are only involved in one task (Gorlick, 2009). Of course, students won't believe this information when teachers or parents tell them about it; they are going to need to read about it and perhaps do some tests of their own. Creating and executing a study of multitasking in middle schools and drawing conclusions from their results would be a great advisory activity. They could even publish their conclusions on the Web at Voice Thread (http://voicethread. com/#home). In any case, students (and perhaps some teachers) will need help as they learn to balance the lure of the Web and social networking with the required work at hand. Pontificating will not do the trick; students will need hands-on learning for this topic.

6 **As a team update yourselves on the current copyright rules.** Students cut and paste images and pull music from the Web with little thought about the intellectual property rights of the creators. Further, the fair use and attribution rules are complicated. However, it is just as important to teach students about where they can get images and music without breaking copyright laws as it is about plagiarism of text. There is a whole new dimension of publishing called Creative Commons licensing (http://creativecommons.org). People who publish using a Creative Commons license often give others permission to use the information, images, and music as long as attribution is provided. Work with your librarian/media specialist to make sure everyone knows the rules of using Web materials on assignments, projects, and presentations. Teachers, too, need to model these practices in their own teaching. Here are some sites to explore with your students:

- Images

  Flickr (flickr.com) Not everything here is without restrictions, so read the small print.

  FreePhotoBank (www.freephotobank.org/main.php)

  Open Clip Art (www.openclipart.org)

- Music

  Legal Music for Videos (Creative Commons) —this site has a long list of places to visit (http://creativecommons.org/legalmusicforvideos)

  Garage Band on Apple computers —students can easily create their own music.

Just remember all of these places are public spaces so it is important to chat with students about what to do if inappropriate things should pop up.

7 **Explore iTunes U** (www.apple.com/education/itunes-u). iTunes is a free download no matter what type of computer you are using—PC or Apple. This site is just *totally awesome* as the kids would say. It is so immense it's hard to describe—there are audio and enhanced podcasts and videos from universities, K-12 organizations, and sources beyond academia. Almost every topic imaginable is here. Resources for teachers, for students, and for the public in general are gathered for general consumption, and they're free! Learn about a public school in Australia, study Islamic banking, view the *Beautiful Universe* from Harvard University, or look at the exhibitions at the Tate in London.

8 **Prepare a parent media/Internet education program**
that the team can use during parents' nights, conferences, and in newsletters. Many parents are understandably reluctant to have their children use computers at school. They often act out of fear because of the horror stories they've heard or seen on TV. Parents and community members need to be educated about digital learning, just like the students.

A site you must check out has already done much of the prep work. Common Sense Media (www.commonsensemedia.org) is a non-profit, non partisan group whose mission is in part "... dedicated to improving the lives of kids and families by providing the trustworthy information, education, and independent voice they need to thrive in a world of media and technology." They offer reviews and information on all aspects of media and technology. Part of their site is dedicated to education, and they have an entire free parent media education program. Topics include: Internet safety, digital citizenship, social networking/virtual worlds, and mobile/communicating. Of course, the team should investigate the website and look closely at the materials before using them. It certainly is a good resource for planning the team's approach to this huge topic.

Often when programs on the media are offered at school, few parents show up. Parents lead busy lives and an additional meeting even on such an important topic may not bring in many participants. Teams need to think strategically about ways to disseminate this information. Can this topic be discussed during curriculum night? Is there a stand-alone handout that might be given out at a basketball game or concert when many parents are in attendance? What topic might be included in parent conference night? Are there items that might be made available through the public library or on the school's website? How can the team help students and their parents have calm conversations on this topic? All generations have to become more knowledgeable about media in all its forms, and a team is in the best position to shepherd this educational process along.

Next Steps

1 **Design a formal licensing test that students must master before they can take ownership of their device.** Students have to demonstrate that they understand the importance of stewardship of their laptop or hand-held tool and are fully conscious of their responsibilities for the machine.

Figure 7-1. Student license for technology device

Technology License

_____ has demonstrated that s/he understands the responsibilities associated with having this _____ assigned to him/her. _____ also agrees to comply with the school rules and to use the device only for schoolwork.

Machine #

_____ Signature

The license test should include questions about critical operating procedures, using the school server, storage and charging processes, information on practices that can slow their machine down, and downloading protocols. The test can be written, oral, or have both written and demonstration portions. Obviously, it can be taken as many times as necessary to achieve mastery quickly and efficiently. This device is a valuable learning tool, not a reward, so it's important to get them into all of the students' hands as soon as possible.

2 **Form an iTeam of students to assist in managing the devices,** help teachers and students troubleshoot when something doesn't work well, and on occasions, teach team members shortcuts and new programs. Team teachers have to work with the school technology people to train students selected for this team. Sometimes iTeam members help school personnel produce videos and presentations. Taking time to develop such a team is a beneficial investment because calls to the Tech Department will decrease when there are students on hand able to problem solve on the spot. Think how helpful it would be to have someone handy to help out when the computer screen image and the LCD projector image do not match, or when all the students in a class are making their first movies, and there are more questions than the teacher can possibly answer. Because the iTeam members do not have the administrative password, they cannot change anything that will cause problems or damage. The iTeam is a school-tested strategy; middle and high schools across Maine use iTeams and even have a conference just for the iTeams' members at the University of Maine (www.maine.gov/mlti/studentconference/index.shtml).

3 **Hold regular "Show and Tell" sessions at all-team meetings** or during advisory where teachers and student share neat digital tools they have learned about and perhaps used for personal projects. Students are exploring Web 2.0 tools on their own outside of school, and it just makes sense to use their expertise in the classroom. Watching an Animoto slide show (http://animoto.com) of a team member's rafting trip down the Colorado River will build general knowledge as well as spark interest in the tool. Follow up with reflection questions such as "What's special about that tool? What does it allow you to do that you can't do now?" Then ask the question that requires everyone to think of adaptations for that tool. "How might we use that tool to demonstrate what we've learned in our classes?" Then the team teachers really should incorporate some of these tools into their instructional plans. The students will be intrigued and pleased as the teachers start using their ideas!

4 **Commit to the students to try one new digital tool per marking period.** Give students some power in making the decision by allowing them to vote on which of three tools to use. If you are hesitant or nervous, make sure the choices are relatively easy to integrate into the curriculum such as: use webcams to make observations of the natural world (www.earthcam.com), take a virtual field trip (www.theteachersguide.com/virtualtours.html), or listen to a podcast. These tools do not require the teacher to create anything, just set up the LCD projector and have a plan for integrating the material into the lesson. If on the other hand, you like to jump in with both feet, explore the possibilities of using Skype to interview experts on a topic in whatever unit is being studied, join an ePals global project (www.epals.com), or create animations on xtranormal (www.xtranormal.com). Allow students to offer suggestions on ways to incorporate digital tools into their classes—they'll have plenty of ideas. It's all right not to be the expert when using digital tools. The students are likely to be much more at ease with them and will gladly teach others how to use them. Teachers need to allow themselves the freedom and joy of being fellow learners with their students as they explore these extraordinary learning tools.

A last word from Jill...

Jill wants to be sure you realize that schools where every student has a personal computer at hand all day every day will soon be the norm. It is happening all over the world, not just in the U.S.

Many readers may feel that the prediction that every student will soon have some sort of digital device may prove true elsewhere but never at their schools. It's hard to imagine that resources will be allocated for technology when there aren't enough desks for students, and the copy paper runs out in February or sooner. However it is interesting to note that many of the places instituting one-to-one projects are not necessarily wealthy areas. What happens is that a leader, educational or political, realizes that this type of project will benefit both the students and the community by providing access to tools and resources that help students develop sophisticated skills needed in the global economy. Once that vision for teaching and learning is formulated the hard work begins. The leader(s) then must exhibit steadfast courage in the face of ferocious opposition to stay the course, and they must identify people to lead the project that understand it is about learning and not the hardware and software.

Even though readers may feel this scenario is a fantasy in their district, eventually a tipping point will occur when more districts than not have this type of project online. The districts lagging behind will realize that one-to-one computing is not an "add on", but an "instead of" that changes the way students learn. Hopefully readers will want to find ways to hasten the arrival of 21st century learning in their schools and will push their school community to move forward.

This major advancement is not to be feared, but embraced. Get ready. Take time to do some upfront study and planning. Come visit us in Maine—we'll give you a five star tour of one-to-one computing!

8

Use the Internet to Connect Your Classroom to the World

Helping students become informed consumers and users of all the Web offers is a huge task and an exciting opportunity for teachers to open the world to their students. A team approach will both increase student skills and help teachers get a handle on the rapidly changing reality of the Internet.

Digital Research Traps
Await the Unwary

Three students are working around a table in their science class. Their task is to choose an endangered species to research and then craft a policy statement to state legislators designed to ensure that the species endures. They are trying to agree on what species to focus. Willy has found an interesting site with lots of information and multiple links. Let's listen in on their conversation.

Willy: It lives in the Pacific Northwest forests—that's near us. It would be fun to learn about it.

Tim: Maybe we can even submit our proposal to the legislators down in Olympia. Does this site have the info we need? Habitat? Predators? Food?

Zack: Look, here's a map of where it lives. But you know, I've never heard of it before. Do you think this is a good site?

Willy: Sure it is—look, here's a menu and links. And frequently asked questions. It's losing its habitat because of logging and suburban sprawl. We've been reading about those problems.

Tim: This is cool—they change color when they are angry. I've seen its relative do that down at Seaworld. It was really cool. And look... here's its Latin name. This site has good information. I think this creature should be our project.

Zack: I don't know; something isn't right. Let's keep reading. Hey guys... look at this under FAQ. It says that Sasquatch is a predator.

There's no such thing as Sasquatch. This is a joke.

Tim: It's not a joke—look at all of these links! And there's a picture.

Zack: Guys, there is no such thing as a Pacific Northwest Tree Octopus (http://zapatopi.net/treeoctopus). Mr. Hayes is just testing us to see if we will really check out this site for reliability before using it for our research. Let's check www.whois.net and find out who owns this site. Bet you an ice cream sandwich it's a fake.

Teaching middle grades students to do research projects well has always been a lengthy and multi-step process. Too often, students were set loose in the library with a stack of index cards and tasked with taking notes, usually resulting in their copying word-for-word from an encyclopedia. As the experience of our three student researchers above illustrates, learning to research today is even more complex because of the vast array of information available at everyone's fingertips. Heck, folks can't even agree what to call the research process anymore—*Information Literacy? Information Fluency? Digital Literacy? Digital Information Fluency?* Whatever the nomenclature, the complexities of modern research are here to stay.

Building students' research and inquiry skills is critical because:

- **Locating information, determining its veracity, and applying it has now become a key life skill.** The Internet is used daily to search out all types of information—current events, opinions, car values and prices, movie reviews, historical events, and even the meaning of life (http://aristotle.net/~diogenes/meaning1.htm). Today's access to digital information is democratic with equal access for all (as long as you can afford the devices and correlated fees or have access to a public library). Just as students should understand the rights and responsibilities of living in a democratic society, they also need to know the ins and outs of Internet inquiry. In both instances, the only way to gain a full understanding of the benefits and pitfalls is to practice with knowledgeable mentors offering guidance along the way.

- **Inquiry is important in every discipline.** Questions advance the learners' knowledge of any discipline: *Why is the character responding in such a way? How does the gravitational pull affect the tides? What will happen if the slope is increased in this graph? Was the American Civil War inevitable?* Furthermore, when students approach a unit or lesson through inquiry, they become more engaged in the learning because their questions become the focus, and they are finding the answers. Students today simply need to have command of a wide array of research/information literacy/information fluency tools.

- **The process of research /information literacy/information fluency is complex**. The tools of this process need to be modeled and then practiced multiple times in a variety of contexts across the curriculum. Because students need to use them to some extent in every class, it makes sense for teachers to collaborate in building the skills. Collaboration is expedient and it gets better student results.

As the Team Begins Collaborating...

1 **Choose an organizing system that will help the team systematically teach research skills.** Some schools already have a research plan in place, so students receive instruction that builds on previous experience. Of course it's always a good idea to check with the teachers in previous grades to find out what actually was taught as opposed to what the curriculum guide says should have happened. In many districts, research/information literacy/information fluency is approached in a willy-nilly fashion, and students emerge with a hodgepodge of skills and no real mastery of how to work independently through an inquiry project. Fortunately, the team can use their own inquiry skills and find several models and correlating support materials on the Internet to adapt to their students' needs. Yes, this process will take time, especially the first year a team collaborates to design a coordinated approach. However, by using a team folder on the school server or a team wiki, the team can place all of the materials in a central location to which everyone has access. The team can then adapt and add to these lessons as needed. The librarian/media specialist should be the team's number one resource. Unfortunately in these days of budget shortfalls, libraries often sustain cuts that cause irreparable long-term harm to teachers' ability to engage students in meaningful and powerful learning. So if a team is bereft of in-school resources, here are several sites to find information on the critical elements of the research/information literacy/fluency process.

- The Big 6: Information and Technology Skills for Student Achievement (www.big6.com and www.big6.com/kids). These sites are multi-faceted and include some free lessons, descriptions of units in which teachers have integrated the Big 6 components, and free resources such as graphic organizers and note taking templates. This is also a commercial site and offers products and staff development. They take advantage of social networking tools such as Twitter and Facebook, and have a RSS feed. This approach has a process with six components:

    - Task Definition

    - Information Seeking Strategies

    - Location and Access

    - Use of Information

    - Synthesis

    - Evaluation

- Noodle Tools (www.noodletools.com). This subscription site also offers free tools that are extremely useful. Their free tools include "Choose the Best Search," a tool to help identify how to use search engines and their features for efficient searching, and several resources for becoming an expert in the tricky world of citations. There are also some interesting resources for teachers including one with critical information about ethical researching.

- Maine Learning Technology Initiative's Webcasts (http://maine121.org/webcasts). The state of Maine is in the eighth year of its learning technology project, known affectionately as MLTI, or the laptop project. In 2009 the project initiated a series of webcasts that tackle issues related to integrating technology, including the research process. Anyone can sign up for a webcast; all that is needed is a computer and a phone. Plus all of the previous webcasts are archived and can be viewed at one's convenience.

- ISTE Standards (www.iste.org/AM/Template.cfm?Section =NETS). Published by the International Society for Technology in Education, these standards are related to the entire world of the integration of technology into education and are worth a close look. The third standard relates directly to research and information fluency: *Students apply digital tools to gather, evaluate, and use information.* Students

  - Plan strategies to guide inquiry.
  - Locate, organize, analyze, evaluate, synthesize, and ethically use information from a variety of sources and media.
  - Evaluate and select information sources and digital tools based on the appropriateness to specific tasks.
  - Process data and report results.

- 21st Century Information Fluency (http://21cif.com). This is a commercial site that was originally connected to the Illinois Mathematics and Science Academy. There are free tutorials and wizards that help both the budding and accomplished searcher become even more proficient with information fluency skills. Many students often feel because they use the Internet so much that there is nothing new to learn. The search challenges on this site will test the skills of each and every student.

- University of Maryland University College (www.umuc.edu/ library/tutorials/research/intro.shtml). Although this site is designed for older students, it has resources that are useful to teachers. It is divided into seven modules: Doing Research, Copyright, Using the Library, Call Numbers, Finding Books, Finding Articles, Finding Websites.

Once the team has identified the steps they will use to teach research, they should look for places in the curriculum where there is a natural fit. Every assignment does not have to include the entire research process. Some assignments may only include locating resources and evaluating them for reliability while others may focus on taking notes, paraphrasing, and summarizing. Team teachers can divide these skills and teach them in the context of their own curriculum units. Creating a plan that sequences the skills in a logical way will provide students with adequate practice so that eventually they feel competent to complete the steps independently. When assigning multi-step tasks, teachers shouldn't forget to chunk them up into segments with checkpoints in order to monitor student progress (see Chapter 4).

2 **Commit one team meeting a month to explore together research/information literacy/information fluency tools on the Web.** Use an LCD projector to shoot the sites up on the big screen so everyone can see them. If teachers all have laptops, bring them, too, so that all the teachers can follow along on their own devices. Team time is the perfect opportunity to provide some focused professional development for one another. The students may know more and be faster than most of their teachers when it comes to Internet use. So what! It's time to get past the fear of *not* being the only expert in the room. If team teachers can figure out enough about a Web tool to introduce it to the students and explain that everyone in the class will help each other become an expert, then collaboration and problem solving are being modeled in an authentic way. A simple directive such as "OK, I've got you started, now one of your jobs is to teach me something I don't know about this tool or site" works well to engage students. The students will think that is a great challenge, and they will rise to the occasion—especially if there is a little prize associated with teaching the teacher something new. Everyone wins—the students learn about a new tool; the teacher becomes more proficient; and each time she teaches the lesson it becomes a bit more comfortable. So what are some useful research/information literacy/information fluency sites the team might explore?

- Citations: These are murderous to teach and it seems the rules change regularly at the whim of authorities like APA and MLA. Rather than teach the rules, it makes sense to spend time teaching why citations are important, what needs to be cited, and which sites show how to do it correctly.

    - Noodle Tools: www.noodletools.com
    - Son of Citation Machine (http://citationmachine.net)

- Essential questions: *This We Believe: Keys to Educating Young Adolescents* calls for curriculum that is "challenging, exploratory, integrative and relevant" (NMSA). One big step in achieving that all-encompassing goal is to transform the traditional research project requiring students to merely regurgitate information into an inquiry project requiring students to actually synthesize information from several sources and offer original thinking. All inquiry starts with a good question, which is not always a snap to generate. Here are a couple of sites to explore:

    - http://tinyurl.com/questions123
      (an article by Grant Wiggins)
    - http://tinyurl.com/questions124
      (a site devoted to inquiry)
    - http://tinyurl.com/questions125
      (an article by Jamie McKenzie)

- Organization: After students finish their research, they are left with a lot of information to sort through, synthesize, and organize. There are a variety of tools that will help them through these processes. If team teachers each take responsibility for one tool, students benefit by becoming proficient with several Web-based organizing strategies.

    - Thesis Builder (http://tommarch.com/electraguide) helps students build a thesis statement or plan a cause and effect essay.

- Bubbl.us (http://bubbl.us) allows students to build and download webs that will help them organize and synthesize information they want to include in a presentation or project.
- Persuasion map from ReadWriteThink (http://tinyurl.com/persuasion123) helps students organize their notes into a persuasion essay.

- Social bookmarking: Most Internet users bookmark favorite sites. More and more people are using social bookmarking sites because it allows them to share and access interesting sites. What a great strategy to use when students are working on group projects. They can share resources across their group, their class, their team, the country, and the world. Students are probably familiar with these sites, so it's a logical step to help them harness these tools for group work. If one worries that students might post inappropriate sites in the name of schoolwork, the teacher can set up the site and have students e-mail the sites to post. Of course, before using any of these sites, teachers need to check them out for appropriateness and security.

  - www.portaportal.com
  - http://delicious.com

- Wikis: These websites are free and provide a team or an individual teacher a great tool for collaboration by providing online workspaces. Teachers can closely control access to these tools by making them open only by teacher invitation. Many such sites allow teachers to monitor all the posts before they can go live. Students use wikis for a number of research purposes: generating ideas, sharing resources, asking questions, rehearsing arguments, and giving and receiving feedback.

  - http://pbworks.com
  - www.wikispaces.com/site/for/teachers

- Interesting search engines: Everybody googles! But Google presents sites in a linear fashion. However, there are more visual ways to search the Internet that may appeal to some students. They are interesting to play around with. Visit:
  - http://search-cube.com
    The site comes up in a visual cube that can be manipulated.
  - http://search.yippy.com
    Yippy organizes the search results into categories.
  - www.bing.com
    This engine helps you narrow your search.

Next Steps

1 **Use activities to help students learn how to evaluate the reliability of a website.** This is a critical component of any research or inquiry project and should not be skipped. *November Learning* (http://novemberlearning.com) is a treasure trove of lessons focusing on information fluency and is easy to use. (In the menu at the top click on Resources and then Information Literacy Resources.) These resources include ideas for using the resources in class and provide links to other useful sites. The resources include how to read a website URL (what do .com, .edu, .net, and ~ mean?), how to figure out who owns the site, and how to access the history of a website. It also has links to sites similar to the Northwest Pacific Tree Octopus that the three students at the beginning of the chapter were perusing. Plus, titles like "California's Velcro Crop under Challenge," "Dog Island Free Forever," and "Dihydrogen Monoxide, the Common Beverage Additive That Can Be Dangerous to Your Health" intrigue and interest students while giving them insights into the unreliability of many websites. Teachers also will learn a lot from these resources. Once students understand the purpose of checking out websites, the steps can become part of the sequence students use as they begin any inquiry or research a topic for any class.

Other evaluation materials available on the Web are "ready-to-go" and often teacher-created and downloadable.

- What's It Worth?
  (www.albany.edu/~ef8043/introquest.htm)

- Jurassic Park: An Information Literacy Webquest
  (http://fayette.k12.in.us/~cbeard/jp/webquest.html)

- ReadWriteThink lesson on evaluating websites
  (http://tinyurl.com/evaluation12)

Remember that modeling the evaluation of a website once is not enough. Students need to see that all of their teachers value this critical skill of effectively reviewing a website, and they need multiple practices before it will become second nature.

2 **Introduce students to the concept of inquiry and research with an activity that requires no computers, just paper and pencil.** A typical inquiry approach to teaching has four components: (1) answering a question that may not have one right answer, or solving a problem, (2) collecting data/information, (3) analyzing the information/data, and (4) drawing conclusions and/or arriving at solutions and then presenting them (Worksheet Library). It's a relatively straightforward process to turn a traditional report or project such as "Your Favorite President" into an inquiry project by framing it as "Why Has History Forgotten Franklin Pierce? or "How Might United States History Be Different If JFK Had Survived?" However, students used to collecting as much information as possible and arranging it attractively on a foam project board or in a PowerPoint may be uncomfortable with the challenges of analyzing information and drawing conclusions because getting an A or B will now be based on demonstrating critical thinking skills. A wonderful activity called Convivial Research will build students' understanding and comfort with the unquiry process. This activity incorporates many elements that motivate students—a topic that they are passionate about, a chance to work with peers, an opportunity to chat with everyone in the room, and a platform on which to take a stand. It is also low tech, easy to implement, and requires very few materials. However, it does require a great deal of thought on everyone's part. Here's the process:

Figure 8-1. Convivial Research Process

Convivial Research Process

Part A

1. A few days before the activity, ask the students what topics they have strong feelings about—music, food, the best media stars, etc. Generate a list on a large chart and then have students put stars next to the topics that most appeal to them. When everyone has posted stars, the topics with the most energy will be evident.

Pizza ✱✱✱✱✱✱✱

Action Movies ✱✱✱✱✱

Hot Stars ✱✱✱✱✱✱✱✱✱✱✱✱✱✱✱✱✱✱✱✱✱✱✱✱✱✱✱

Ghosts ✱✱✱✱✱✱✱✱✱✱✱✱✱✱✱✱✱✱✱✱✱✱✱✱✱✱

Super Bowl ✱✱✱✱✱✱✱✱✱✱

Best Bands ✱✱✱✱✱✱✱✱✱✱✱✱✱✱✱✱✱✱✱✱✱✱✱✱✱✱✱✱✱✱✱✱✱✱✱✱

Desserts ✱✱✱✱✱✱✱✱✱✱✱✱✱✱✱✱✱✱✱✱✱✱

---

2. Based on the number of stars, pick the topics to be the subject of the Convivial Research. In the group above, desserts, best bands, ghosts, and hot stars generate a lot of interest. It's important to let the students put stars next to all of the topics that interest them to increase the probability that one of their topics will be used.

3. This next step may be completed by (1) just the teacher, (2) the teacher and a group of volunteers, or (3) the entire class. Turn the topics into open-ended questions. So a question about the best band isn't simply "What's your favorite band?" but something like... "What are your criteria for liking a band, and who meets those criteria?" Or "Which was a better music decade—the 60s with the British Invasion or the 80s with the advent of *Thriller* and other music videos? Why?"

4. The day of the activity, post the research questions so that everyone can easily read them, and have paper available for students to write answers to the questions. A visual tweak to this activity is to use a variety of colored construction paper cut into hexagons that students later use to create a quilt for display.

Part B

- Working with a partner, students select a question to research.
- The pairs circulate among their classmates and ask the other pairs of researchers to respond to their question.
- Pairs record the answers they receive on their hexagon. (They should not answer their own question.)
- They should answer other groups' questions in turn.
- Encourage all pairs to keep moving, spending no more than a few minutes with each other.
- All pairs may not get fully around the room, but they should interview as many other pairs as they can. Try to allow at least 20-30 minutes for these interviews.
- Pairs then meet with other pairs who researched the same question and chart the gathered information.
- After looking for trends and patterns in their data, they draw one or two conclusions to share with the class.
- The research groups report out to the entire class or team.
- The teacher then asks everyone to reflect on the process.
  - How was this process different from just reading about a topic?
  - How was the content of the report-out of the results different from a traditional content of a poster, report, or PowerPoint?
  - How might we adapt this process to our project work?
- This concrete research experience can be referred to when the group next tackles an inquiry/research project.

This activity generates a lot of energy with students. It works well with a single class, but can be even more fun when done at the same time with the entire team. Find a space large enough for all of the students, and wheel in an overhead or LCD projector to project the research questions up on a blank wall with the questions large enough to be read by everyone. The benefits for doing a Convivial Research activity with the entire team include:

- Helps to build a sense of community among the entire team. Because students seldom get a chance like this to interact with everyone on the team, this is a unique opportunity to appreciate the diverse nature of classmates' life experiences. Each student has a similar experience at the same time. There is no "We did it this way in Ms. Lange's class," or "Mr. Cavanaugh said this," when referring to the process in another context.

- Builds goodwill as students appreciate their teachers' recognizing they like to work with their peers.

- Sends a strong message of what type of learning all of the teachers on the team value and that there is an expectation students will actively create new learning using their inquiry and processing skills.

These ideas were adapted from Convivial Research at www.promiseofplace.org/assets/files/Convivial%20Research.pdf

3 **Be bold, go where no other team at your school has gone before—bring the experts to your students via the digital communication capabilities of the Internet.** Imagine the benefits. Students meet and chat with people from other cultures or with experts on a topic they are studying. This kind of personal contact engenders lifelong interests and helps students think more deeply about issues and concepts than if they are just abstract ideas in a text. In the last century although teachers often provided students opportunities to interview members of the community for research projects, it was difficult. The necessity to leave school and miss other classes plus transportation issues often became insurmountable challenges. Now, Web applications like Skype, Gmail, and iChat all have videoconference capabilities that can bring the experts right into the classroom. A team can organize time so that the chat can take place with a small group, a class, or the entire team. These applications do come with their own challenges. Many districts block Skype and other chat sites and are adamant that these sites present a danger and opportunities for students to get into trouble. What to do?

Barbara Greenstone, a statewide integration mentor for Maine's MLTI laptop project offers this advice, "Don't ask for access to a specific application because it's too easy to give reasons why it won't work on the school's system. Instead explain your instruction purpose and let the tech folks develop the solution" (B. Greenstone, personal communication, January 18, 2010). Using this advice as a foundation, a team should put together a plan that explains what they want to do and why it is important to their students' learning. It makes sense to include examples of other schools involved in similar activities. Take this request to the administration and the Tech Department well in advance of the launch date of the inquiry project. Also include the names and positions of the people with whom the students would like to communicate and details about how the communication will be monitored. Then ask for permission to go ahead. Framing the request as an instructional issue rather than an access issue might just break open the digital blocks. Involving students in this type of research that brings the world to the classroom is becoming more and more common.

School to School:

- Students in Bill Ivey's Humanities class at Stoneleigh-Burnham School in Greenfield, Massachusetts, connected with students at The Children's Storefront School in East Harlem via Skype. Stoneleigh-Burnham is an all-girls private school, and Bill's class was pursuing an inquiry focusing on the question "Are girls smarter than boys?" They were looking for other students with whom to collaborate. In his article detailing this collaboration in NMSA's *Middle Ground*, Bill describes the process the two schools used. Through an education listserve, Bill found a partner in Steve Bergen, a computer teacher at The Children's Storefront School. Using a laptop with a camera at each location, students at the two schools communicated through Skype video chat. The partnership extended beyond the original inquiry unit to include Web design and a cross-state writers' workshop focusing on poetry. This exemplifies how educators are harnessing the power of technology resources to match their students' needs with those of educators in distant locations. Listserves, such as MiddleTalk for members of NMSA, connect educators across the globe.

- ePals (www.epals.com) Here's how ePals describes itself:

  - ePals is a global community of collaborative learners, teachers, and academic experts in 200 countries and territories.

  - ePals provides connections to students, classes, and school districts worldwide that are safe and secure.

  - ePals is the safe and protected solution for linking classes, schools, and school districts globally via ePals SchoolMail™, ePals SchoolBlog™, and Classroom Match.

Students have opportunities to communicate and work on collaborative projects with classes half a world away. There are both ongoing projects to join and opportunities to work with another class to develop an original project. E-mail capabilities are included at this site as well as forums for teachers, students, and families.

Invite the experts in!

- Electronic Emissary (http://emissary.wm.edu) is a site dedicated to connecting mentors with interested students. This site supports educators setting up projects and provides guidelines for the mentors. One project on the site is a Stars and Constellations project. (http://tinyurl.com/experts123). The instructor reports,

  The weaker students gained a lot of self-confidence as they learned to ask questions and received respectful answers from the online mentor. Their computer and telecommunication skills improved. Student engagement remained high throughout the project, and students didn't want it to end. Parents commented positively on the impact on their children.

- Students in Lisa Hogan's science class in Topsham, Maine, were able to discuss global warming with scientists in the Antarctic who were collecting ice cores to track climate change. After finding their names in magazines and newspaper articles, Lisa contacted the scientists. She did have to do a bit of Internet research to locate e-mail addresses, but people she contacted at universities and organizations were helpful in passing information along between the scientists and students, who often brought in articles they thought would help the group with their project. Her students had school accounts, and Lisa wanted them to think of these accounts as "work" accounts rather than personal accounts. She views her smartest step as having her students interview their parents or other relatives about how they use e-mail at their work sites, which led the students to recognize the differences between work and personal e-mails. After she checked their initial e-mails to the scientists for spelling and grammar, the class had conversations about the importance of such things in "professional" communications. Further learning about the importance of digital communication and collaboration skills came from the requirement that they cc both her and the members of their group on all e-mails. This contact with professionals researching the topic of global warming provided Lisa's students with authentic data that was not filtered through a political lens. Their work had meaning.

- Webcams: Live cameras are continually focusing on a myriad of subjects: aquariums, famous landmarks, animals in the wild, and building projects. Google webcams to find one that fits in with a unit. Using their observational skills, students can gather authentic data for their inquiry as it happens in real time. Although watching animals at a waterhole in Africa is not quite as authentic as being there, over time it provides students with quantitative data that they themselves can collect. Webcams are just another tool provided by the Internet to make inquiry engaging and meaningful in ways that help students to understand their world and make the topics under study relevant.

One last word on research—Provide students with authentic audiences for the presentation of their projects. Teams come with ready-made audiences. Social studies Period 1 can invite the math class in; Period 2 can invite the language arts class in; and so on. In addition, invite parents and community members, and possibly plan an evening presentation to accommodate those who work. Having to present to an audience other than their class builds in a higher level of accountability for students. However, it is important to point out that if a team does opt for authentic audiences for presentations, they need to provide students with the scaffolding to create cracker-jack presentations. That means instruction and practice. These take time, and a team has to come to consensus that they all value this type of learning because it means time will be taken from specific content instruction to provide the necessary time to teach students presentation skills. These skills are basic in our participatory, democratic society, and have not generally been well-taught.

Here's how one team from Amherst Regional Middle School in Massachusetts taught their students presentation skills:

- Students did an inquiry project in science and had to prepare to present their findings to a mixed audience of peers, family, and community members.

- The team set aside a block of time each day for a week to prepare students.

- They invited the drama teacher to come in and lead exercises focusing on speaking and eye contact.

- The art teacher came in to teach students about preparing visuals. So that the varied socioeconomic status of the students did not impact their access to materials for visuals, all of them were done at school.

- In extended homeroom periods students practiced their presentation with a partner. Then partners joined with another pair, and they practiced again. Groups were joined again so that students practiced in front of a larger group. The teachers were roaming through the groups offering suggestions and encouragement.

- Eventually it was "show time!" The students were prepared with quality visuals and several opportunities to rehearse and receive feedback before the final assessment.

  M. Hayes personal communication, April, 2005

This team made a conscious decision to be innovative and teach intensely the art of presentation. They understood that if they were going to require presentations, then they needed to value them by providing adequate time and instruction to help students master the process, which paid off many times over.

A last word from Jill...

- All teachers share responsibility for teaching students how to effectively use information literacy skills and helping them become astute consumers of Internet information. Curriculum must be adapted to include a heavy dose of information literacy skills in every class.

- Using motivating tools such as social networking and Web 2.0 tools to involve students in powerful and meaningful learning is good teaching. Because students use these tools outside of school every day, it makes sense to use them in school, too. A recently released book by William Kist entitled *The Socially Networked Classroom* promises to be a good resource for teachers.

- Because the world of information literacy changes so rapidly, we must recognize that lessons may have to be revised yearly. No longer can lessons on the Dewey Decimal System and the card catalogue be used over and over again. These wonderful opportunities to try something new will help us keep curriculum and instructional practices from becoming stale and static.

9

Integrate Ideas and Skills Across the Curriculum

21st Century citizens must be flexible thinkers able to see connections among events, ideas, and processes to creatively solve complex problems. Opportunities need to be provided for middle school students to practice these critical skills. Generating their own questions that drive integrated curriculum units is one excellent way to provide these experiences.

What Class Are We In?

"Let's grab our lunches and get settled. After we eat, we'll have each learning group give a progress report on their work." Team 8B settled in to eat and socialize atop a grassy knoll on Swan Island overlooking the Kennebec River. The whole team had ferried over earlier on the Department of Inland Fisheries and Wildlife launch and had spent the morning exploring the island. Each learning group had a specific task to complete related to the integrated learning project they were working on. All students in Maine are required to study Maine history, and the teachers of 8B decided to use Swan Island as a focal point of the unit because its history, geography, geology, and economics are a microcosm of the state of Maine as a whole. The team had crafted this essential question as a focus for its study: "How does the history of Swan Island reflect both the history of Maine and the contemporary issues facing our state?

As a bald eagle soared overhead looking for his lunch and several white-tailed deer bounded off into nearby woods, Ms. Lange and Mr. Cavanaugh called the team meeting together. "First, let's police the area and make sure we are carrying out everything we brought in. Who's got the garbage bags?" Joyce, Jeannie, Julia, and Ginny pulled several large green garbage bags out of their backpacks and started circulating among their teammates to gather up the lunch detritus. Each learning group had a task that ensured this field trip would go off without a hitch.

Rich and Winnie assumed center stage because they were the student leaders for today's team meeting. "We have the order of the learning groups' progress reports listed on this chart that Rich is holding," said Winnie. "First up is the group specializing in the major historical events connected to Swan Island followed by the group studying the changing economics of the Island. If you look at the chart, you can see when your group is up."

Rich then reminds everyone of the team norms for presentations. "Let's all give attention to Landon, Lamont, Ming, and Jane as they report out. Remember our Big 3: eye contact, no side conversations, and helpful questions."

Landon begins summarizing their project, "We're looking at how big events in American history were connected with Swan Island. Today we're working on the Revolution because Benedict Arnold stopped at the island along with Aaron Burr on their way north to invade Quebec. We wanted to try to figure out where they landed, where they camped, and other things. We've been reading diaries and even Kenneth Robert's novel Arundel to find clues. We got some great pictures of possible sites for our iMovie. Our next steps include drawing a map of the island and the surrounding towns and locating possible sites of events related to the Revolutionary War. We have more questions, too—why did they stop here and not on the banks of the river near a town? And who were the Native Americans that the expedition ran into on the island? Why were they on Swan Island? Did they help Arnold and Burr find their way to Quebec?"

The report-outs continue. Students ask their classmates good questions that will help them dig a bit deeper into their topic. The teachers busily take notes, identifying which groups need a little extra coaching and which ones seem ready to move on to the next steps in preparing for their projected Swan Island exhibit. At the end of the presentations, Mikey, a towhead who hasn't hit his growth spurt yet, madly waves his hands and arms for attention. When called on, he blurts out, "You know I really like this unit and what we're doing— not just this field trip, but everything. But what I don't get is—I mean, I never know what class I'm in. Everything we study is connected somehow; the work is fun, but it's so different from... well, school!

His teachers just smile and say, "That's just fine; keep up your hard work" (www.maine.gov/ifw/education/swanisland/index.htm)

179

Some readers are likely to respond to the above scenario by saying that they could never do such a project in their school because they have to prepare for tests, and their district curriculum lays out exactly what they have to cover. Unfortunately, such thoughts are understandable. Teachers who must use a scripted curriculum or adhere to an inflexible one where everyone is on the same page on the same day all over the district may find it nearly impossible to develop curriculum units that integrate content and standards in two or more disciplines. On the other hand, such explanations may be a rationalization covering fears and apprehensions. Some see integration as an "add-on" rather than an "instead of;" others believe integrated units can't provide the necessary introduction and reinforcement of specific skills or the direct teaching needed. Finally, and honestly, many other teachers fear giving up the power to control absolutely the content and activities of the unit means that they will not be able to address the necessary standards. Given the pressure educators are under these days, this thinking is understandable. However, despite any apprehensions you may have concerning curriculum integration, I hope as you read the following pages you will find a path that will lead toward integration—which you have been itching to try.

First, let's clarify and define curriculum integration. Beane (1995), its leading proponent, points out that curriculum integration is not an organizational arrangement so much as it is a way of thinking about what schools are for, about the sources of curriculum, and about the uses of knowledge" (p. 616). Brazee and Capelluti (1995), who are also noted advocates, offer these views:

> Integrative curriculum is based on a holistic view of learning and recognizes the necessity for learners to see the big picture rather than to require learning be divided into small pieces. Integrative curriculum ignores traditional subject lines while exploring questions which are most relevant to students. As a result, it is both responsive to students' needs and intellectual because it focuses on helping learners use their minds well (p. 10).

Nesin and Lounsbury (1999) say curriculum integration has these four essential characteristics:

- Students and teachers collaboratively plan the curriculum and how it is pursued.

- Themes provide the organizing center for learning activities. These themes are derived from students' interests and concerns.

- Learning tales place in a democratic classroom community where everyone actively participates in decisions.

- Separate subjects no longer define the curriculum. Personal concerns of social significance become the main focus of learning (pp. 1-2).

Another way to frame integrated curriculum is in terms of Real World Learning. Google "Real World Learning" (RWL) and over 58,000 hits come up. Mike Muir, Director of the Maine Center for Meaningful Engaged Learning, uses Real World Learning as an umbrella term to include these five components:

1. Learning by doing
2. Student voice and choice
3. Higher order thinking (apply, analyze, evaluate, create)
4. Real world connections
5. Technology as a learning tool

With the help of these various descriptors, the reader should be able to conceptualize what an intellectually challenging, relevant, and engaging *integrated* unit looks like.

Because there are varying views and interpretations of integration, a team should develop its own common understanding of what they mean when talking about "integrated curriculum." The team's having a clear grasp of what they believe about this approach will ensure their planning goes smoothly. Discussing how such a unit differs from a more traditional interdisciplinary or discipline-specific unit will help the team sharpen their concept. They must address how an integrated approach benefits students now and in their futures, how standards will be met, and what the drawbacks might be. Some activities to help teams build a full and common understanding are

- Watch the video entitled *Challenge Based Learning* on YouTube. It takes you step-by-step through designing an integrated unit that uses a community challenge as a basis. It's informative and fun to watch. www.youtube.com/watch?v=fOii_YyJQGA

- View *Applying Math Skills to Real-World Problems!* www.edutopia.org/mountlake-terrace-geometry-design-video. Although this is one teacher creating a math experience, it has many of the attributes of an integrated unit. Pay special attention to how this teacher asks community experts to give feedback to her students.

- Read "Visualizing Technology Integration: a Model for Meeting ISTE Educational Standards" at www.edutopia.org/ferryway-school-saugus-ironworks and view its accompanying video, www.edutopia.org ferryway-video. Notice how this integrated unit expanded beyond the traditional interdisciplinary team to include the allied arts.

- Explore the Maine Center for Meaningful Engaged Learning webpages, www.mcmel.org/web/Home.html

- Read the little book, *Curriculum Integration: Twenty Questions—With Answers*," by Nesin and Lounsbury. In just 60 pages everything you have always wanted to know about curriculum integration—well almost everything—is provided.

- Discuss NMSA's Position Statement on Curriculum Integration, which is available from NMSA's website. (http://tinyurl.com/integration123)

Why your team should institute integrated curriculum—in the words of practitioners:

- "The power of ownership should never be underestimated." This principle of enduring importance was the first of sixteen identified in a powerful last chapter, "Lessons Learned: What Experience Taught Us" in Alexander's book, *Student-Oriented Curriculum*.

Rules, curriculum, content, and assessment measures take on new meaning when they belong to you. This point was driven home time and time again as we interacted with these sixth graders. It was an incredibly refreshing experience to work with kids who were enthused about what they were doing. Their growth in academic achievement, behavior, and willingness to take responsibility for their own learning was inspiring. They exceeded our expectations in all areas, primarily because of the fact, we are convinced, that they saw what they were doing as "theirs" (p. 55).

This short but adequately detailed book provides a map for getting started with integrated curriculum.

- "Integrated programs are useful in tracking other areas of concern" (Carr, p. 14). In teaching any unit any time in middle school, a team is addressing a myriad of objectives and issues—some are academic, while others are more social. Teams must think about

    - How will we address all-school goals?

    - How can we better support students' transfer of standard grammar conventions to subjects other than English?

    - Are we seeing an upswing in cliques and bullying?

    - How might we get our students involved in the community?

    - How can we demonstrate that heterogeneous grouping increases learning and achievement for all of our students?

    - How can we help our students see connections between this unit and their lives?

The team's planning together of a unit provides time for concentrated talk about the whole-child issues as well as academics. Integrated units provide unique opportunities to address goals and skills that cut across the curriculum as well as weave in activities that address the social and emotional development of the students. Teachers worried that students don't apply skills they have learned in one class to the work they do in other classes can build in multiple experiences for using those critical skills in a variety ways in an integrated unit.

An example of a team addressing a social issue through their unit content is a team using Carl Hiaasen's book *Hoot* in their integrated unit on the environment. The story line surrounding an antagonist trying to help save the habitat of the endangered burrowing owls while dealing with a bully provides many entry points for a team to address both academic and social issues. Read Dennis Carr's *Getting Started with Curriculum Integration*, another quick read that provides steps as well as inspiration.

- Student achievement improves in an integrated curriculum. There is a substantial body of research and documented practice, both old and new, to support this statement. Students are not adversely affected academically by integrated curriculum. In fact the opposite is true—students do as well or better on standardized tests as their peers in more traditional settings.

    - The Alpha Team (Kuntz, 2005), which has been practicing a multiage, student-centered program for nearly forty years, reports that "Over the eight years of using these tests (The New Standards Reference Exam), Alpha students outscored their counterparts in Shelburne (VT), the Chittenden South Supervisory Union, and in the state" (p. 112).

    - Mark Springer (2005), who has been practicing integrated curriculum for decades, has documented that while his students take the standardized tests along with other students, curriculum integration has never inhibited his students' abilities to succeed on high stakes standardized tests. Considerable detailed documentation supporting that judgment is provided in *Soundings*.

In addition to succeeding on standardized tests, students benefit in other important ways due to the nature of integrated curriculum (student voice, big questions without easy answers, and group project work). Students

- Make connections among concepts and ideas.
- Practice problem solving and information literacy skills.
- Become adept at working collaboratively, a major 21st century skill.
- Learn to become self-directed learners.

One more excellent reason to implement curriculum integration comes from the world of brain research. David Sousa (2006), who writes extensively about brain research and its application to teaching and learning, makes the point that "transfer is an integral component and expectation of the learning process" (p. 138). There is much evidence that shows most students are not able to transfer ideas, skills, and concepts from one situation to another which indicates new learning has not been internalized. Sousa goes on to say, "Successful transfer can be enhanced by educators who advocate thematic and integrated curriculum. This approach provides more stimulating experiences for students and helps them see the commonalities among diverse topics, while reinforcing understanding and meaning for future application" (pp. 138-139).

Student buy-in, the ability to incorporate multiple issues and concerns, increased learning, and internalizing new learning for transfer to future situations are compelling reasons for a team to integrate their curriculum. Kathy McAvoy, past president of National Middle School Association, thinks there's one more—revitalization of teacher enthusiasm and commitment (Alexander, p. 71). Curriculum integration is a fun and creative way to teach and learn with students.

Baby Steps to Help Teams Begin the Process of Integrating Curriculum.

① **Help your students learn to ask questions.** One would think that asking questions comes naturally to young adolescents, and it does, but in the school setting they have developed a hesitancy to ask questions for fear of appearing ignorant. When the teacher asks, "What questions do you have?" he likely receives blank stares. So provide practice in interesting ways.

- A colleague, Lynn Yuodsnukis, helped her students develop the skill of questioning with the simple, yet provocative statement, "I once saw a ghost." Students would then have a few minutes to ask questions to ferret out the details.

- Teachers at Massabesic Middle School in Maine are using the "parking lot" technique. They have a white board in their classrooms called the parking lot where students post questions and comments about the day's lesson at the end of the class.

- Professor Edward Berger from Williams College appoints a student to be the "official questioner" at the beginning of a class. He has students' names on index cards and pulls one a day. That student's job is to ask several questions throughout the period. This process seems to liberate the other students and they then begin to ask their own questions.

2 **Begin to experiment with mini lessons.** Most language arts teachers recognize the term "mini lessons" that has evolved out of the reading-writing workshop approach to middle grades language arts and has been perfected by Nancie Atwell. Briefly, a mini lesson is short, focused lesson on a specific skill or concept. Usually the teacher models the skill or process, provides exemplars, and invites students to give input into the lesson. In language arts a teacher might be teaching how to write a strong lead. However, this technique can be used in any subject. For example, a social studies teacher might teach students how to mine a census document for information or a science teacher might teach classifying skills in a mini lesson. Becoming proficient at crafting and delivering mini lessons prepares teachers to deliver skill and process lessons during an ongoing, integrated project.

3 **Help your students think in an integrated manner.** Outside of school everyone thinks in an integrated manner, but in school the tendency is to use subject labels to define thinking. The problem-solving skills of math class do not transfer to science lab. Try this strategy in advisory or homeroom. Bring in a snowboard or a skateboard and engage everyone in conversations about the sport. Model thinking out loud as you point out all of the subject knowledge that intersects for one of these boards to be designed, manufactured, and used in a competition. Then bring out a popular CD or DVD and have students work in small groups to brainstorm similar information about producing this item. Find interesting events or products on the Internet and go through the process regularly in advisory or homeroom or as a sponge activity in classes. Giving students opportunity to practice thinking in this way prepares them for the innovative thinking they will do later when tackling a multi-faceted issue of an integrated unit.

4 **Allow students to explore different ways to demonstrate what they have learned**. Making multiple products is an attribute of differentiated instruction that should be a natural part of middle grades instruction. However, many educators are reluctant to take this step. The key is to be crystal clear about the content and skills that will be assessed by first creating an assessment list or rubric with these criteria. Then expand the list or rubric to include the criteria for the specific product whether it be a poster, iMovie or podcast. Make sure the content is weighted most heavily in the lists or rubrics, unless, of course, creating the product is the main task. A terrific resource for teachers looking for ideas on what to include in rubrics for different products is http://rubistar.4teachers.org This site has multiple templates that can be adapted to specific needs.

5 **Choose the content.** Identify where in the curriculum it makes sense to integrate. View an integrated unit not as an addition to the curriculum, but rather as a different way of studying content. Mark Springer suggests that there are several ways to incorporate mandated curriculum within an integrated unit.

> As a rule, however, because all knowledge is ultimately interrelated, teachers can use the content information they are required to cover either directly, when that information coincides with student questions, or indirectly as case studies, background, or parallel examples to illustrate the students' questions. Any topic area about which students ask questions has a history, for example... if a teacher has to cover a certain historical period, he can look at the students' topic as it existed in that time period and then have students explore similarities and differences with the present. Similarly, there are always scientific connections to every set of questions, and I've yet to have students raise a set of questions that wasn't reflected in some literature and other art forms. After all, art is a human response to questions, and the questions students ask are not "new" to anyone but them. What we're really saying here is that knowledge is naturally integrated. Only in schools do we isolate and segregate

knowledge. Yet, by tapping into the natural integration of all knowledge through the students' questions, the students gain a connection to the required content through their own interests, and learning and retention increase.

Personal communication, July 7, 2010

The first time a team uses student questions to help develop a unit they will be amazed at how closely student questions align with standards. Look at this list of questions students generated in Dennis Carr's unit on global warming (p. 33):

- What is global warming?
- What will happen if the sun burns out?
- How does global warming happen?
- Can you see global warming?
- Is global warming toxic?
- How do people affect global warming?
- Does global warming have any color?
- Is global warming a gas, liquid, or solid?
- Can you breathe it?
- Does it affect the atmosphere?

Compare these questions with his state standards below. There is plenty of opportunity to craft activities that help students answer their questions and ensure that they address the state standards in several different subjects:

- Science: *Ecology, Continuity and Change, the Earth, the Universe, Energy, Inquiry and Problem Solving, and Scientific Reasoning*
- Visual and Performing Arts: *Creative Expression*
- Health: *Influences on Health*
- Social Studies: *History*
- *Language Arts: Process of Reading, Informational Text, Process of Writing and Speaking, Standard English Conventions. Research-Related Writing and Speaking*

- Math: *Data Analysis and Statistics, Patterns, Relations and Functions*

Other things to consider include: Are there community resources that fit better with one unit than another? When won't standardized testing interrupt you? Is the weather a consideration? What mandated material must you include?

Also check out what other schools have done for ideas and inspiration:

- Bath Middle School: http://bath.memorynetwork.net
- King Middle School: http://king.portlandschools.org/files/onexpedition/onexpedition.htm
- Skowhegan Area Middle School: www.msad54.k12.me.us/sams/projects09/main.shtml
- Edutopia's Problem-Based Learning module: www.edutopia.org/project-based-learning

6 **Plan!** Recognize planning an integrated unit for the first time will take more time than expected. As the team becomes more adept and at home with the process, the process will become second nature. Here are some steps and resources to help:

- Edutopia has an entire section on planning project-based learning units. These steps work well for almost any integrated unit. www.edutopia.org/teaching-module-pbl-how

- Essential questions are often a key element, and they are not easy to write. Here are a couple of websites that give pointers.

    - Big Ideas: Authentic Education e-journal http://tinyurl.com/essentialquestions123

    - The Question Mark: http://questioning.org/mar05/essential.html

- Assessment *of* learning needs to be built into the overall unit plan. Be crystal clear about the skills and knowledge that will be assessed. Fuzziness about this aspect of a unit invites criticism that the units are just fluff and do not represent "real" learning. Make sure the criteria for assessing mastery of a standard or skill are made public when developing a summative or final assessment. Some schools have peer review teams that help unit developers clarify their thinking about purpose and outcomes; this extra step ensures the quality of any type of unit.

- Assessment *for* learning strategies is also a critical component. Decide what techniques the team will use to check on student progress (formative assessment) and how the team will differentiate for students who need more or less time to master the skills and new knowledge. Anne Davies (http://annedavies.com) and Dylan Wiliam (www.dylanwiliam.net), two experts who offer classroom-tested ideas, provide the type of information teachers need to adjust their instructional plans to meet student needs.

- Incorporating student voice in the curriculum planning process is a critical component. The books cited in this section describe different processes in detail. A two-page planning process for achieving curriculum integration developed by Jim Beane is included as an appendix in the book *Curriculum Integration: Twenty Questions—With Answers*.

- Technology integration should be integral to the unit plan. Web 2.0 tools, media production programs, and research capabilities provide the team with flexibility in planning.

- The different learning needs of the team's students need to be considered while planning, not afterwards as an add on. All of the books and articles of Carol Ann Tomlinson, a former middle school teacher, offer specific, classroom-tested teaching strategies. The team should also familiarize themselves with Universal Design principles of the Center for Applied Special Technology (CAST), which include using

- Multiple means of representation, to give diverse learners options for acquiring information and knowledge.

- Multiple means of action and expression, to provide learners options for demonstrating what they know.

- Multiple means of engagement to tap into learners' interests, offer appropriate challenges, and increase motivation.

Check out the CAST website for more information on Universal Design (www.cast.org/about/index.html).

7 **Look for sinkholes.** Find a trusted colleague who has an eye for detail and run the unit plan past him or her. Some forgotten detail or unintended consequence can scuttle a great child-centered learning experience in a flash. Identifying potential problem spots ahead of time can save a lot grief and frustration. Also, be sure the team consults with specialists and special educators about the best ways to include their students and meet their needs. Their expertise will make the unit stronger.

8 **Implement and keep a journal or blog**. Take notes during any integrated work so that the team can reflect on what went well, how students reacted, or what might be tweaked next time. If a team's work is to improve, they must take time to reflect. Schools are beginning to acknowledge the critical role of reflection with the institution of professional learning communities. Also, the next year when it is time to recreate the unit, the team's notes will trigger fresh, relevant work.

Don't obsess about the "right way" to do an integrated unit! Experiment! Nowhere is it written that an integrated unit has to last for a set amount a time or slavishly follow an exact process. Perhaps a team will try a one-day integrated experience just to see how it goes.

**A last word
from Jill...**

In closing, I want to share a few more comments from Mark Springer on the topic of integrated curriculum collaboratively designed by students and teachers.

- Using student questions to frame units and lessons automatically makes the learning authentic for the students. They discuss their questions and concerns rather than the teacher's. This, in turn, increases students' motivation to learn and to develop the skills required to address their questions and articulate answers.

- Rather than isolating and segregating knowledge, tapping into the natural integration of all knowledge through students' questions connects them to the required content based on their own interests, and their learning and retention increase.

- A tangential advantage comes in the form of teacher-student relationships. By honoring their questions through sincere investigations, teachers build rapport and respect with the students. This, along with the intrinsic motivation described previously, goes a long way to reducing the management/behavior issue in a classroom.

- Other advantages include the ability to differentiate "instruction" more authentically when using students' own questions and having them help find and present answers. By empowering students to assist in all phases of the learning, which they will be happy to do when the topic addresses their own questions, they can more readily use resources appropriate to their abilities (and often want to stretch themselves to try new ones!), to develop skills, and to find ways to present information that best match their individual strengths and talents.

Personal communication, July 7, 2010

10

Connect the Dots that Link Differentiation, RTI, and Formative Assessments

---

School systems are notorious for layering initiative upon initiative. Often these initiatives are facets of a plan designed to address a major overall problem. Unfortunately the plan sometimes is not known or understood by staff, students, and parents. Teams can work together to identify the commonalities among these initiatives and collaborate in meaningful and strategic ways to ensure their students meet standards

---

Grappling with Response to Intervention (RTI)

The team gathers around the table looking at the latest data on their students' progress. They are experimenting with reformatting the twice weekly study halls into focused six-week skills blocks that address the specific learning needs of their students.

Fred, the team leader, summarizes the decisions just made and looks ahead. "Here's what we have so far: (1) Melanie is going to continue to use the time for her pull-out program in reading, and (2) we're going to address three skill areas plus provide enrichment for students already meeting all of the standards in those three areas. We've decided on two skills blocks so far—measurement and inferences. The enrichment block will be designed with the students' help. So, which of these other areas of concern should we also address? Understanding the scientific method? Paragraph development? Vocabulary development? Constructed responses?"

"We have a huge number of students who are not doing well on the constructed responses," replied Celeste. "I wonder whether we should delay addressing that skill until the next six-week block, and then focus on constructed responses with everyone and do follow up practicing in our classrooms." Heads nodded in agreement.

"I know the scientific method will show up on the state test. Plus we're working to include more inquiry-based learning across the curriculum. They both require similar kinds of thinking. I think it would give the kids' skills a real boost up in all areas of the curriculum if they internalized the scientific method this early in the year." Another round of agreement.

"I have an idea for the measurement group I want to bounce off of you," said Fred. We've all agreed that in the skills blocks we probably need to use different instructional methods than we use in our classes. More of the same only louder isn't going to help our students master the standard. So...I was thinking about adapting Trail-O precision orienteering ideas. Students would have to use precise measurement—we'll practice using the metric system; they would have to use the scale on the map, and we could take different types of measurements along the trail!"

Lamont chimed in, "Hey, can I come along? You're absolutely right. We have to think differently about our instruction in these skills blocks as we address the RTI requirement to meet the needs of students not mastering the required concepts. I'm thinking about using popular media and webpages to model and practice making inferences."
I'm also beginning to think that I should be planning my instruction differently in my regular classes, too. Maybe there are ways to help more students master the concepts initially so that an intervention is not necessary.

This team works in a school with no extra resources to hire additional staff to meet the requirements of RTI. The only resources they have are themselves and their common planning time. The entire school is committed to a literacy-across-the-curriculum initiative. They have great expectations this initiative will help to decrease student-reading problems and thus lower the number of students who need RTI in reading over the next several years. The reading initiative plus an ongoing commitment to differentiation are evidenced by changes in the instructional practices of the staff. The teachers are integrating assessment for learning techniques into their instruction as they work to become more adept at differentiating. During common planning time the teams discuss the different initiatives, look for the ways they are interconnected, and exchange ideas on adapting their curriculum and instruction to incorporate these new practices.

It is important to integrate learning initiatives because...

- **Achieving academic success is job one, and connecting initiatives will improve students' learning.** The report *Turning Points 2000, Educating Adolescents in the 21st Century* (Jackson and Davis) makes it very clear that ensuring the success of every student is the primary responsibility of the middle school and called for schools to

  - Teach a curriculum grounded in rigorous, public academic standards for what students should know and be able to do, relevant to the concerns of adolescents and based on how students learn best.

  - Use instructional methods designed to prepare all students to achieve higher standards and become lifelong learners (pp. 23-25).

National Middle School Association's *This We Believe* (2010) defines student success far more broadly than just doing well on state tests. "Thriving now and in the future requires becoming a lifelong learner and demands more than a basic understanding of reading, writing, and mathematics. It requires the ability to apply sophisticated skills in a variety of settings and solve complex problems individually and in collaboration with others" (p. 4).

Middle level position statements have led the way in calling for educational practices that make sure *each child* is equipped with the skills and knowledge necessary to take advantage of all that life offers. In the 2010 report "Gaining Ground in the Middle Grades: Lessons from California," Williams and Kirst state that those schools that have "ensuring the success of every student" as part of their mission have been effective. "The schools are oriented to the future and take every opportunity—and an all-hands-on-deck approach—to get all of their students on track to succeed in high school and prepare for college." The report goes on, "The district's role is to set the standard and provide the resources; the principal's role is to drive the focus on student outcomes and manage and orchestrate the school improvement process; the teachers' role is to *improve their own practice, but also work collectively to identify the students needing help and get them the intervention they need"* (www.edweek.org). Teams are in a unique situation to work collectively to identify students needing help and get them the intervention they need. Differentiation, RTI approaches, and formative assessments, along with other initiatives have the same desired outcome—ensuring all students' success.

- **Helping students and families fulfill their responsibilities for student achievement is a daunting challenge.** Successful schools "communicate to students and their families that they, too, are responsible for student learning and outcomes by attending class, turning in homework, trying hard, and asking for help when needed" (Williams and Kirst). However, as Cathy Vatterott points out in *Rethinking Homework*, there is a continuum of the level of parent involvement in supporting and helping children with their homework from none to the over-involvement of hovering helicopter parents (p. 35). There is strength in numbers, and a team can send a consistent message to their students and families. Of course, just sending the message is never sufficient to effect change; the team needs to communicate in several ways to explain standards, differentiation, and RTI. Working together, teams can build trust with parents to help them understand how the various programs and resources will benefit their children as they morph into teenagers who respond and act in new ways.

- **Understanding how each school initiative is connected to the others is difficult but important to figure out.** Picture a juggler with six balls in the air labeled RTI, differentiation, new math program, literacy across the curriculum, formative assessment, and backward design. Notice that the juggler only can have his hands on two of the six balls at the same time. That's what it is like for teachers who deal with multiple initiatives as separate entities, an approach that saps their energy. Now picture teachers holding one ball constructed of six interwoven bands labeled with six initiatives, each supporting the others. Remove one band and the ball becomes weaker; remove another band and the ball collapses. Reframing multiple initiatives as one multifaceted initiative with a single purpose ensures success for all students and helps everyone stay focused on that purpose.

Team teachers can help one another identify the ways the different initiatives work together to support student learning and achievement. How can a team connect differentiation, literacy, formative assessments, and RTI? Teachers have to be adept at using formative assessment techniques so they know when and how to differentiate and who to refer for RTI. The International Reading Association's Guiding Principle #1 for RTI reads, "Instruction: RTI is first and foremost intended to prevent problems by optimizing language and literacy instruction" *(Reading Today)*. Differentiation often revolves around literacy issues; even a math program can be difficult for students if they are unable to comprehend the text. A team's multiple perspectives can frame a big picture that helps the team members optimize their instruction and can allow the team to think creatively about time and space.

Ways to
Plan Together

1 **Know your students really well.** Design a system that ensures the team has periodic discussions about each child. It may be as simple as each week having the team review a portion of a stack of cards with a card for each student, or perhaps the team works its way through a list with everyone making his or her own notes. Maybe the team creates a digital system. Whatever the system, student confidentiality must be protected. Anything digitally produced on a district machine should probably be considered open to public scrutiny. These discussions should focus on information that helps teachers differentiate. Here are some examples of teacher input that, when shared, will help other team members plan accordingly:

- Bobby uses story boarding as a prewriting strategy in my English class. Once he sees things visually, he is usually successful in putting his ideas into words. I bet that strategy would work as a way for him to organize his thoughts in his other classes, too.

- Brian likes to dismantle small engines at home I learned today in advisory. When I talked to him about this hobby, he said he just likes to see how different parts work together. So maybe using a mechanics metaphor will engage him in other topics.

- Ali still struggles with reading. So in her classes she will need either alternative texts, recordings, or directed reading prompts that help her sort through what's important and what's not.

- Lloyd seems to work better on a big space like a white board than on notebook paper. Maybe his fine motor skills are still developing. Anyway, letting him work on a white board and then taking a digital picture of it might work for some assignments.

- Libby is a really strong audio learner. I let her brainstorm orally and record it on her computer. Then she slips on headphones and works from her recording.

Not only is it important to be reviewing student learning strengths and challenges to differentiate, but also to spot potential problems before they become crises. Providing students with a short, focused intervention that improves a specific skill or rectifies a misperception can short-circuit a downward spiral leading to failure. With multiple people noticing and noting information about the students' learning processes, a team becomes responsive more quickly to cognitive issues as they present themselves.

② Create a visual map that shows how the team is implementing various mandated initiatives. Often the realities of the school day transpire at such a rapid pace that teachers have no time to reflect on what they are doing and why they are doing it. Then suddenly it's time for a parent conference, an observation by the principal, or a share time at a faculty meeting. Questions start flying about what is happening in the classroom and why it is happening in such a fashion. If the team has taken the time to map out what they have been doing in a simple way, team members have time to reflect on their practice and look for connections across the team that are working or need to be refined. This kind of reflection gives teachers thoughtful, concrete information to share rather than responding off-the-cuff in a less-than-cogent way. It can be a very simple map or web.

Figure 10-1. *Example of a visual map of a team's plan*

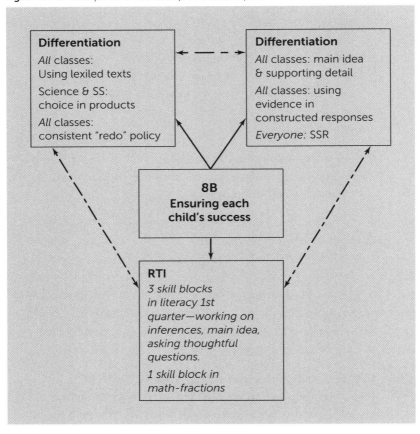

By creating this simple web, the team provides themselves a visual representation of how they are connecting the various mandated initiatives. It gives them talking points in meetings with others, provides a focal point for their own reflection on how well things are going, and gives them an image to share with students as they talk with them about the purpose of different techniques, flexible grouping, and assignments being used. Teams update the map or web at the end of each quarter or trimester, which provides a record of their collaborative efforts throughout the year.

Here are some helpful online resources for differentiation, RTI, and formative assessment.

Figure 10-2. Online resources for differentiation, RTI, and formative assessment

Response to Intervention (RTI)	• National Center on Response to Intervention: www.rti4success.org • Dr. Carol Tomlinson's webpage: www.caroltomlinson.com
Differentiation	• National Center on Response to Intervention: www.rti4success.org • RTI wiki designed for middle school: http://middleschoolrti.pbworks.com
Formative Assessment	• Anne Davies: http://annedavies.com • Dylan Wiliam: www.slideshare.net servusuk/dylan-wiliam, http://tinyurl.com/DylanWiliam or Google "Dylan Wiliam"

Next Steps

1 **Use minute-to-minute and day-by-day assessment for learning techniques.** The following information demonstrates the critical importance of formative classroom assessments of learning and achievement (Wiliam, 2007). Researchers compared three instructional changes in practice and their resulting growth in student learning over time. As the chart below shows, the greatest growth in student achievement was linked to the incorporation of formative assessment as a regular instructional practice.

Figure 10-3. *Results of changes in practice over time*

Change in practice	Increase of learning gained in a year
Reduction in class size from 30 to 20 students	3 months
Boost teacher content knowledge from low to high	1.5 months
Formative assessment	6-9 months

Formative assessment, sometimes called assessment for learning, is a powerful force in the campaign to improve student learning and achievement. There are a variety of models, and the one advocated here focuses on the minute-to-minute and day-to-day assessment of student understanding of the material being studied. Dylan Wiliam of the University of London describes formative assessment in this manner: "Evidence about student learning is used to adjust instruction to better meet student needs; in other words, teaching is *adaptive* to the student's needs, and assessment is done in real time" (p. 191). These are not assessments that go in the grade book but rather give the teachers information on whether they can move on or need to reteach. What do they look like? Here are several from Wiliam and other sources:

- Quick questions with dry erase boards: Each student has a dry erase board or a stack of scrap paper that will be recycled. Ask a question that checks for understanding that can be answered quickly. Picture a unit that has been focusing on producers, consumers, and decomposers in an ecosystem. A quick prompt such as "Write down two decomposers in the forest by the time I count to five" gives the teacher immediate feedback. If the answers are Lady Slippers, pine needles, and fallen branches, the teacher knows immediately that reteaching using a different strategy is necessary because the first strategy didn't work too well. It's important not to ask questions that students can easily answer correctly just by guessing.

- Two-minute summary: give students two minutes to respond to a prompt that will give evidence of learning. They are just used for gathering information about what students understand and are never graded. Examples are

  - Write all you can remember about photosynthesis.
  - Make a list of every Spanish word you know.
  - List the parts of a science lab report.
  - Create five algebraic expressions.

  The above examples are all recall. Use verbs like *diagram, organize, compare, contrast, categorize, prioritize, rate*, or *select* to craft two-minute summaries that require a higher order of thinking:

  - Categorize these eight animals as vertebrates or invertebrates.
  - List all the ways fractions and decimals are similar.

- Traffic light signals: each student has a stack of three paper cups—one red, one yellow, one green on the corner of the desk. As long as the green cups remain on top all across the room, the teacher knows the lesson is going well. Yellow and red cups signal there are questions and confusions. The teacher has visual evidence that she needs to adapt the instructional plan. When this strategy is used across the team, students just come to accept it as part of class; they are more intent on listening and don't hesitate to indicate when they are confused.

Effective differentiation demands minute-to-minute, day-to-day assessment if the goal is to meet students where they are and scaffold their learning so they can internalize the knowledge and skills they need to meet standards. This type of assessment is also critical to an effective RTI program. Intervening quickly when a child is struggling is important so that the student can get back on track as soon as possible.

These techniques seem to be relatively easy to implement. However, they often require a teacher to change long-standing teaching practices. Experienced teachers have established definite patterns of instruction during their careers. If those patterns do not include gathering evidence of learning throughout a unit and then using that information to adapt instructional plans or to give feedback to students on specific next steps to take, the teacher faces a learning curve regarding formative assessments. As stated previously, one of the magnificent benefits of teaching as a part of a team is the collegial support it provides. Teammates can share formative assessment techniques that work, offer ideas for refining them, and use similar approaches across the curriculum so that students internalize procedures and thus focus on the content. All of this sharing happens on a daily basis, not once a month at a staff meeting or professional development event. Finally, using formative assessments helps the team tame the multiple initiative nightmare by having evidence of learning on which to base decisions about RTI, differentiation, and other mandates.

2 **Give feedback with specific next steps to students and parents.** Knowing what to do next to meet a standard is a vital component of successful differentiation and targeted instruction. Individually teachers provide this type feedback in their classroom on individual assignments. Dylan Wiliam's research shows that giving specific feedback increases achievement more than just giving grades or giving grades plus feedback (Wiliam, 2006). What is descriptive feedback? Typical feedback does not give the student enough information to know either why he is successful or what specifically should occur to improve the quality of his work. Without such information the student cannot transfer strategies to another situation. Here's a chart that shows typical feedback and then how it can be restated to be more descriptive.

Figure 10-4. *Comparison of typical and descriptive feedback*

Typical Feedback	Improved Descriptive Feedback
You need more details about this character.	How might you use things the character *says* or *does* to provide evidence to support your statements?
Check your steps in problem solving.	I notice you have been clear about defining the problem. Then you jump right to your solution. You need to go back and include how you decided what the key issues were and then possible solutions.
Great Lead!	Your lead is very strong because you hook the reader immediately by jumping right into the action.
Incomplete—Redo.	Your PowerPoint has • Introductory slides • Concluding slides • 3 big ideas You're missing • Statistics to back up ideas 2 and 3 • A slide of Works Cited

The team can generalize this practice by meeting with students and/or parents to have conversations about district curriculum assessments and standardized tests. Again specific strategies should be discussed and perhaps mini-plans of action decided upon. For example, if reading fluency is an issue, the team might suggest in a family conference that once a week the student choose an interesting Internet article and practice reading it several times at home. Then at the end of the week, she reads the piece to an adult at home. The teacher encourages the adult not to get hypercritical, but to emphasize improvement in the child's fluency. Unfortunately in too many homes there is no one to play this supportive role, so the team needs a fallback plan. Perhaps there's an adult in the school who can help out, they set up a peer partner from another grade (reading aloud to younger children is a great way for middle grades students to build their fluency), or the advisory teacher can be the listener. The goal is for students to receive guidance in steps they can take to improve identified skills. Students need to see that they are making progress over time. Periodic teacher-student conferences to discuss specific skills progress should occur. These can be scheduled during homeroom, at lunch, or even during class. The point is that the team demystifies test scores for students and shows them ways they can take responsibility for their own learning. Providing specific, descriptive feedback that a student can use is the critical step.

3 **Develop a plan for "do-overs" that everyone on the team uses.** Grading, late work policies, and whether or not to let students resubmit work are topics that often lead to very spirited discussions. When a team frames their work around the concept of ensuring success for all students and believes in a "whatever it takes" approach, it becomes obvious that individually assessing students as they work toward mastering a standard is a different process than tallying points in a grade book. The former suggests that there are different paths students may take to meet the standard and that time is a variable. The latter process of accumulating points is often subjective and relative, and time is rarely a variable. The traditional practice is to grade down work with mistakes and to apply penalties to late work. The opportunity to redo work to bring it up to higher level for full credit is rarely an option. One argument is that this is not what happens in real life. That argument is rubbish. Life is full of do-overs:

- One can take a driver's test multiple times. If it takes three tries, the driver is not restricted to driving for just one-third of the year; he gets a "full-credit" driver's license.

- An aspiring lawyer is allowed to take the bar exam multiple times. Her certificate does not say, " This lawyer deserves only a partial fee because she took the exam twice."

- During the process of applying for a commission to become a notary public, the author misread part of the regulations and missed a question on the exam. The Secretary of State's office sent a nice letter suggesting she reread the appropriate section and resubmit just the answer to that question. The commission was awarded without a penalty for taking two times to "meet the standard."

Schools are one of the few institutions that levy penalties for not being perfect the first time. A team-wide do-over policy allowing students the opportunity to improve their work without penalty sends a message that the teachers recognize that mastery is the goal even if takes multiple tries and that perseverance is an important habit to develop. "Ah!" the reader might be thinking. "Won't that type of practice lead to students being lazy and waiting to do the work at a later time?" It might, but as Rick Wormeli has discovered, "My students realize that they are going to have to do it sooner or later, they might as well do it now and save themselves the time and hassle later. This is what mature scholars do!" He further elaborates eloquently on the topic of do-overs as follows:

> The greatest preparation for current and future school demands is competence with both curriculum and studying. We only become competent, however, by re-doing tasks or re-studying content repeatedly, not by doing the tasks or studying the topic once during the year. Why would we take this opportunity for competence away from students? Repetition creates automaticity and quick reference in our minds—some of the important stuff of competence. It's far more preparatory for students to have multiple attempts at mastery, each with full credit given so there is hope, rather than a single attempt and the teacher's admonishing finger wagging at them when they fail in that first attempt. This is

a false sense that we're building moral fiber here—we're not. Several cognitive science writers claim it takes 24 times of doing something to achieve a consistent 80% competency regarding that thing. When was the last time we did 24 persuasive essays? We can't do this in the factory models of schooling we have today. Teachers who don't allow retakes are trying to protect the pedagogically unsound conveyor belt that doesn't teach. We're there to teach students, counter to the current school culture as it may be. If teachers were treated to this same policy of getting only one chance to learn and to demonstrate mastery of a new skill, they would rebel.

R. Wormeli (personal communication, March 13, 2010)

For a delightful and relevant read on the use of do-overs, secure a copy of *Mr. DeVore's Do-Over. A Little Story for Teachers.* NMSA, 2005.

It also makes sense for the instructional plans to include student/peer assessments that ensure the work is ready to turn in and thus decrease the need for do-overs. Be proactive and provide time for sufficient revisions and practices ahead of a deadline. Dylan Wiliam suggests a technique he calls "Pre-Flight Checklist" (2007, p.194). Just like a pilot has a checklist to go through before taking off, students have a list of the quality criteria for each component of the assignment that need to be met before work is turned in. Until a peer has checked off each criterion as complete, the work stays in the metaphorical hanger for more fine-tuning. Many readers are thinking, "I do that and the students just check things off whether they are present or not!" Try this—have students highlight or underline evidence of the criteria on the rough draft and sign the peer editing sheet. If the draft is computer-generated, students can use the underlining, text color, or highlighting features. Require that students turn in the multiple drafts to demonstrate they have indeed revised and edited. Building in this type of accountability helps keep students intellectually honest.

The point of differentiating and RTI is to provide those different pathways to mastery and success. Being able to do-over and improve the quality of one's work based on descriptive feedback is one of those effective pathways. A consistent policy across the team helps create a climate characterized by high expectations and a belief that each student can meet those expectations. Team teachers must keep in mind the end game, success for every child. Old constructs have to be examined through that lens and let go when they no longer apply!

4 **Actively work to build students' confidence and their belief in themselves.** Ron Clark, author of *The Essential 55* and the subject of a TV movie *The Ron Clark Story*, spoke at a National Middle School Association Annual Conference. An energetic speaker, he described his class in New York City that everyone else just wanted to forget. These students had never experienced any type of academic success and were considered unteachable. Flummoxed at first and not knowing what to do, he taught them how to treat each other with respect. He taught them to shake hands with a firm grasp and to greet people appropriately by name—while working on their academic skills. He used all of his creativity to design ways to engage his students. By enlisting the help of the cafeteria staff to quiz his students on spelling when they went through the line, his students practiced their words multiple times. Slowly the class's behavior turned around, and they began to see themselves as learners. Eventually they succeeded at levels no one would have believed possible. Before he could teach them the academics, he had to teach them that they were valuable human beings. A similar story is that of David MacEnulty, the subject of the movie *Knights of South Bronx*. In this instance chess was the vehicle for building students' confidence and belief in themselves that eventually led to their outstanding achievement.

Most teams and their efforts are not going to end up in a made-for-TV movie, however, there is a lesson from these movies and books. When students feel worthless, they don't learn. When they see tangible evidence of their efforts having a positive outcome, then they begin to engage in academics and make real progress. Sometimes going beyond differentiated lessons and targeted instruction to provide out-of-the ordinary experiential learning opportunities pays huge dividends. It might be a commitment to chess. Or it could be any number of other things: student written and produced plays, community service, math team, double-dutch jump rope, photojournalism using digital cameras or phone cameras, etc. Teams have the opportunity to join forces to investigate these types of explorations and provide life-altering experiences for their students.

A last word from Jill...

Learning does not occur in little self-defined boxes. It spills out across the curriculum. If a child has difficulty reading novels in language arts, she is going to have difficulty reading texts in everyone else's class, too. When teams collaborate to address the skill areas that impact all subjects, they can focus their efforts on strategies and approaches that will provide the biggest payback for the student.

Because many of these topics and initiatives presented in this chapter may be new to your team, take responsibility for your own learning by creating what Brenda Dyck (2010) refers to as Personal Learning Networks. Share resources, explore online together, and provide each other support when trying something new. Start by setting up a team social bookmarking site at http://delicious.com to store and categorize all of the sites the team runs across in their Web surfing. The information will be there 24/7 for everyone.

Students' lives are often adversely affected by their scores on standardized tests. If a team truly believes that their mission is to ensure each child's success, then they are facing a complex challenge. The team's thinking together creatively about time, instructional strategies, and curriculum gives them a better chance at delivering on their mission and preparing students for the challenges that lie ahead.

11

Work *Smarter* Instead of Harder

Collaborative activities done well take time,
and with no additional time available to teachers, fresh ways
to communicate and collaborate need to be explored
and put into practice.

So Much to Do, So Little Time!

"Tina, stop! Why are you banging your head against the desk?"

"I can't take it any more—we have had over 40 e-mails in the last two weeks, just about potential changes to the schedule! My e-mail just pinged and there was number 41. Everybody's got an opinion and assumes the world wants to read it. I want the schedule to make sense, but my brain is bursting—I just can't process anything else. This has been my week—obligation after obligation and no time to really think about what I'm doing in class or, heaven forbid, figure out how we will help Andrei, our new student from Romania, who speaks very little English. I have 10 e-mails from parents waiting for me to answer on what work their children are missing, 105 persuasive essays to read and grade, a meeting after school tomorrow to score district writing prompts, three team PETs to attend this week....ohhhhhhh. Do you know I haven't even looked at the new reading program's teacher's resource book in over two weeks, and I have an observation on Friday? Our dear principal will no doubt ask me which assessment tools I'm using, and why I'm not doing more informational reading in language arts. Do you know how boring the nonfiction selections are in that series? The students are completely turned off by them. I found some really great alternatives online, but when I went to duplicate them, the copier had jammed!"

"Don't forget you have detention duty on Thursday. And I bet someone will ask how the team is using the data from the scores of the standardized tests.

"No! Stop! Don't bang your head any more—you'll give yourself a headache! Come on—we'll figure it out during common planning

time. Just because you are the designated language arts teacher doesn't mean you have the sole responsibility for addressing reading issues among our students."

Tina, like many other teachers today, is frustrated. Although she is a dedicated teacher who wants desperately to provide her students with everything they need to learn, she is overwhelmed by the day-to-day demands of her job. Fortunately, she has a teammate who has begun to see that if their team collaborates more on curriculum and instruction issues, then responsibilities will become more manageable. Students will benefit through their coordinated efforts designed to address student needs.

We need to work smarter because:

- **We have a goal that we are committed to fulfilling.** And to do this "The collective ability of the group must improve with time in order to adapt to new challenges—it has to continuously evolve into a quantitatively better operating unit and effectively react as circumstances change..." These words from Baker and O'Malley in their book *Leading with Kindness* are most apropos (p. 22). Teams need to explore fresh processes and procedures, including the use of new technologies, to improve the effectiveness of the team as a responsive and innovative mini-organization. If any group is satisfied with the status quo, they will slip backwards. It is the professional responsibility of a team to chart its course for continuous improvement. A team that thinks that they have everything figured out has fallen prey to a groupthink mentality and will eventually become less effective because they have closed their collective minds to new ideas. Middle grades teams must be the antithesis of groupthink, always seeking ways to do things better for their students.

- **Common planning time is often seen as one component of a school's organizational practices that can be eliminated.** It is susceptible to being cut in favor of more instructional time or to meet the budget. Team planning time becomes vulnerable when teachers are unable to articulate why it is so important to their instructional practices and show how it benefits student learning. It is imperative that teams find ways to use the precious planning time they have in the most productive ways possible and be able to document how they have used it.

- **Only by collaborating can teams meet the layer upon layer of mandates heaped on everyone's plate.** The academic standards alone are so numerous that there is little time to address them all. In addition, many districts are required to have not only a Response to Intervention (RTI) plan for academics but also one for behavioral issues. The list goes on. Add to the mix, the fact that all teams have what Ruby Payne (2008) calls "under-resourced learners", gifted and talented students, special education and 504 students, and others without a particular label means that middle grades teachers are presented each day with a complex mix of students with varied cognitive, emotional, social, and physical needs. Teachers barely have a chance to take a deep breath or a bathroom break, so finding resourceful ways and new tools to stretch the available time just makes good sense.

Try These Strategies to Use Common Planning Time More Efficiently.

1 **Develop digital routines that save time and paper.**
Recreating and repeating information that can be received and retrieved digitally in seconds is a waste of valuable time. However, privacy issues need to be clearly defined. In some cases e-mail and other communications done on an organization's computers have to be open for perusal by organization officials and others. Be sure to know the school and district policies, and do not assume anything written is privileged information. Despite that ominous warning, a smart team uses all of the tools available to make the best use of their limited planning time. Here are several really cool strategies using Web 2.0 tools that give teams almost instantaneous access to ideas they have never heard before! These tools that allow asynchronous

conversations (not happening at the same time—a phenomenon created by Web 2.0 tools, etc.) save an immense amount of time when planning or researching resources.

- For unit and lesson planning

    - Create a post on Voice Thread for Educators (voicethread.ning.com) that outlines your ideas and resources and then asks for feedback. This site is worldwide and is likely to connect a team with others who have done similar units and have ideas and resources to share. Imagine connecting with a classroom 6,000 miles away that will help your students develop world-views on important issues.

    - Join NMSA's MiddleTalk listserve or another similar group. A listserve allows a member to post a question, ask for advice, or join in a conversation. Responses will arrive very quickly and often provide a fresh perspective or a link to valuable information.

    - Open an account on TweetDeck (www.tweetdeck.com). TweetDeck allows participants to research topics. For example, a search for digital citizenship quickly brings up references to the leading resource book on the topic, a slide show on digital citizenship and social media, and a variety of blogs on the topic. Not everything is of equal value on a social networking site like this, however, good stuff does pop up.

- For general organization and team work

    - Create team wikis—one for student use and one just for teachers. Wikis are digital workspaces where people collaborate on projects. One person creates the space and invites others to join. The originator of the wiki controls who has access and what they can do once they are on the wiki. It might be *read only, write*, or *edit*, Wikipedia is the most public wiki and anyone can add and edit the content. A team or class wiki can be much more restrictive. Go to WikiMatrix (www.wikimatrix.org) to compare sites or just check out PBworks.com. It's one of the simplest to use.

- Teacher wiki: As the teacher in the opening scenario reported, in just one month her team had over 40 e-mails pertaining just to one topic. That's a lot of opening messages and possibilities for miscommunication if someone forgets to either hit *reply all* if necessary or hits *reply all* when the message was meant for the eyes of just one individual. Businesses avoid such issues by using secure wikis to share information among themselves and with clients; they post ideas, which are then commented upon in a very transparent fashion. Having such absolutely secure wikis is very costly, but teachers can create private workspaces for free by limiting who has access to the wiki. ***Needless to say, any sensitive or child-specific information should never be put on a wiki.*** Here are a few ideas for using a wiki among teammates.

  - Post checklists for things like field trips, posting grades, or changing the schedule. At a team meeting just pull up the wiki, and the checklist is right there for everyone's reference. One of the most useful things about a wiki is its availability 24/7 for the convenience of individual team members who may have left the directions for posting grades on their desk when they left school.

  - Use it as a "parking lot" for ideas that come up in team meetings that the group wants to remember but doesn't have time to address right then. These ideas remain visible to everyone for future reference and to add to when new ideas bloom.

  - Draft communications for team members to edit. Words are important, and sometimes a team wants to ensure they strike the right tone or are very clear about directions. Drafting the communication in the wiki allows the team to view and revise the draft together using a LCD projector, permits the team's wordsmith to work on the draft anytime and easily share it with the team digitally, and allows others to add ideas should they strike in the middle of the night or on the weekend.

— Create curriculum units on your wiki. Brainstorm, collect resources, connect to important sites, save images, and plan the steps. These units might be interdisciplinary or for an individual subject. By posting the individual subject area units or at least their outlines, teammates may see connections they didn't know existed across the curriculum and be able to support one another's instruction.

— Use the wiki as a brainstorming tool when discussing topics like RTI, scheduling, and homework help solutions. Ideas can be posted, links to pertinent documents and Internet sites inserted, and concerns raised. Using asynchronous conversations gives everyone voice and keeps to a minimum domination by one or two outspoken individuals. Look at the sample wiki below where the team members have had time to think about RTI previous to the first discussion and have posted some ideas to consider. They will be starting from the same place when they have their first face-to-face meeting.

Figure 11-1. *Example of team wiki*

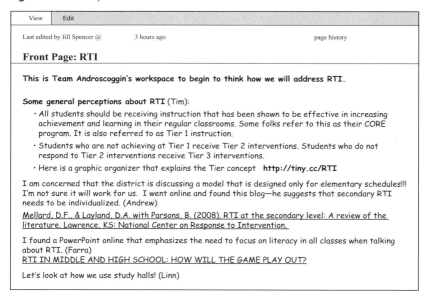

- Wikis designed for student use can be useful for various purposes. Teachers can regulate what gets posted by manipulating the settings they choose. For example, all comments might come through the teacher's e-mail before they can be posted.

  - Knowlton and Wieglus (2005) suggest several ways to use wikis productively with students:

    - Keep students and teachers connected on the days that class does not meet. Ideas can still be exchanged and commented on, and questions can be asked and responded to even when students and the teacher are not in the same room.

    - Block schedules create longer classes in which the teacher often builds in independent work time. Students can use the wikis to collaborate digitally during this time or leave questions or important links for others.

    - Teachers can monitor student thinking and questions through the wiki. They can quickly identify areas where students are having problems. The wiki can be one form of assessment for learning so that teachers know what to do next to increase student learning.

  - Experts in the field of study can be invited to join the wiki, and students can then pose their questions directly to the expert.

  - Assignments can be posted.

  - Students are able to respond to each other's posts. They receive validation from their peers for a good idea and can respond to questions that help them clarify their thinking.

- Save time with e-mail. It also cuts down on paper usage. Team leaders with the responsibility of sharing information given out at the leadership team meeting can share administrivia via e-mail rather than repeating it orally at a team meeting. Be strong and ignore requests at team meetings to repeat the information for folks who choose not to read their e-mail.

- Learn how to do group e-mails so that every name doesn't have to be repeatedly typed in individually. Have one for parents, allied arts teachers, other grade level teams, folks who need to be notified when field trips occur—any group that periodically needs the same information.

- Advocate for student access to school e-mail. Students will often ask a question via e-mail that they will not ask in class. Being able to clear up confusion quickly can head off discipline issues and extra re-teaching time after school.

- Create digital calendars to track important dates and agenda items for common planning time. Many e-mail programs have free calendar functions, as does Google (google.com/calendar).

Figure 11-2.

A digital calendar can help to keep everyone organized and reduce stress. Teams can avoid having to scramble during a team meeting to meet a deadline because it slipped everyone's mind.

- Try Google Docs (http://docs.google.com): Google Docs is another digital workspace to explore. It supports documents, spreadsheets, and drawings and has templates to choose from. Again, using a collaborative digital workspace is efficient because participants can visit and work in it anytime. Imagine that a team is designing its monthly newsletter to send home. Individuals can go in and add material whenever it is convenient for them, the proofreader can edit small increments so he is not overwhelmed at the last minute during the same week that grades are due, and the finished product can be easily transferred to the newsletter template and published on the school website.

There is a continuum of comfort level with digital tools among teachers. There are also access and training issues—the haves and the have nots. If one started teaching in the days of ditto machines and filmstrip projectors, and before calculators, the technology learning curve has been a steady upward slope over the last 30 years. In the last five years that relatively gentle slope has quickly turned into a very steep incline. Often training and demonstrations of practical applications have not been available. As a result there is often a gulf between the younger staff members born digital and some of their more senior counterparts. That gulf can be spanned amicably and fruitfully through collaboration. Senior staff members have a repertoire of strategies and practices, most of which can be adapted to the digital world. The digital natives manipulate Web 2.0 tools with assurance. Combine the two sets of knowledge, and students will benefit. But that is hard work often made more difficult by a techno lingo that sometimes gets in the way. Seeing an application in action is more apt to intrigue people than just reading a description. Here are two strategies for enticing staff to explore the possibilities of the digital world:

- Techno Shows: Bette Manchester (principal) and Barbara Greenstone (tech integrator) devised this approach as a way to introduce staff to the available digital tools. A Techno

Show began all staff meetings. Barbara would create a digital product that demonstrated possible classroom applications. They were short, entertaining, and hooked the audience. They only lasted 10 minutes or so. She then followed up with personal invitations to learn more, with the tech integrator available to go in and work with a team.
(B.Greenstone, personal communication, January 18, 2010)

- Tech & 20: Todd Williamson, a North Carolina science teacher, offers 20-minute sessions after school on various technology topics. These sessions are voluntary and make it easy to meet people where they are on the continuum of technology use in the classroom

Teams might consider advocating for these types of sessions at their school so that everyone has equal access to digital skills and processes. Equal access to a challenging curriculum for students is a mainstay of middle level philosophy. There must also be equal access for staff to the potential of the digital world so that teams can become adept at using innovative and timesaving Web 2.0 tools.

2 **Find ways to support learning in each other's classes.**
There are both skills and knowledge that cut across curriculum areas. By coordinating efforts and using connections across the curriculum, savvy teams can work smarter to support student learning and achievement. Two ways to frame this work is to look at curriculum though the lenses of common concepts and common skills and processes.

- Identify concepts

     Interdisciplinary units provide teachers with opportunities to craft intellectually challenging units that address standards in two or more curriculum areas by focusing on concepts. Often these units focus on an essential question that cannot be answered with a yes or no. *What are ways our town can reduce its solid waste? How have wars advanced science?*

     Multi-subject approach to concept-based teaching is when teachers from two or more subject areas are addressing the same concepts in their class at basically the same time.

Multiple explorations of a concept in a variety of contexts always lead to a deeper understanding of that concept in a shorter amount of time. Here's an example: Think of the concept of "patterns" and the ways it could play out across the curriculum:

  - Social studies—patterns in immigration, exploration, revolutions

  - Language arts—word patterns, sentence patterns, patterns in story development

  - Math—patterns in symmetry, fractals, data

  - Science—patterns in weather, nature, and the earth.

Have each member of the team go through the subject standards and highlight the concepts mentioned. Review the results to find out which concepts cut across all of the discipline standards.

- Identify skills and processes that students use in several classes. Multiple skills and processes are necessary for success in every class. A good example is students citing evidence or examples in almost every class. In science lab they cite evidence to support their conclusions; in social studies evidence is required to back up ideas in project work; in language arts students use evidence in their persuasive essays; and even in math, students provide evidence of their thinking in math journals. Picture a team meeting where Kim, the science teacher, is bemoaning the fact that she just can't seem to get her students to use specific evidence from their lab results to back up their conclusions. Her teammates, sympathetic to her frustration, offer to insert some work on evidence into their instructional plans. The strategies they use will support their own goals and not generate more correcting. Their conversation might go something like this.

  Albert (Language Arts): I can do a 4-Corners activity (Google: 4 corners activity + school) on Friday where I ask the students to choose which of the four characters they think has the most influence on Cassie in *Roll of Thunder, Hear My Cry*. I'll have the names on posters—one in each corner of the room, and students will go to the corner that has their choice of character on the poster. Then I will ask them to develop their case by citing specific events or evidence from the novel to support their opinions. I will be sure to use the word "evidence". This activity will also help me assess the level of comprehension of my students.

Celeste (Math): My students need to do some self-assessment of their math journal writing. We'll take a look at the class wiki together tomorrow and look for "evidence" of clearly written explanations of mathematical reasoning.

Darryl (Social Studies): By next week we'll be ready to do some thinking out loud about what the Bill of Rights really guarantees. I'll use the Provocative Statement approach. The students will respond to a provocative statement with their feet. If they agree, they move to one side of the room and if they disagree, move to the other. Once they have taken their stand, I'll ask each group to prepare an argument to support their opinion using evidence from the work we've been doing. It will be a great chance for them to rehearse their thinking for an upcoming essay assignment.

Kim is delighted that her colleagues are so willing to help out. She can make connections to their lessons in her class and really drive home the idea of using good evidence to support their conclusions.

- Other examples include:

  – History can be thought of as a form of narrative. By using similar graphic organizers in both language arts and social studies, students will have additional practice thinking about universal themes, how people's actions affect others, and the importance of place in both stories and real events.

Notice that the two graphic organizers in Figure 11-3 help the student create a mental picture that draws parallels between the important elements of an historical event with the story elements of a narrative with which they are already familiar. Connecting the unknown (history event) to the known (the way a narrative unfolds) helps the learner internalize new information. Both the historical event and the narrative have important people, some sort of conflict and resolution, and a setting or location. Common graphic organizers provide students multiple opportunities in different contexts to analyze big chunks of information by breaking it down into its critical components.

Figure 11-3. *Social studies graphic organizer*

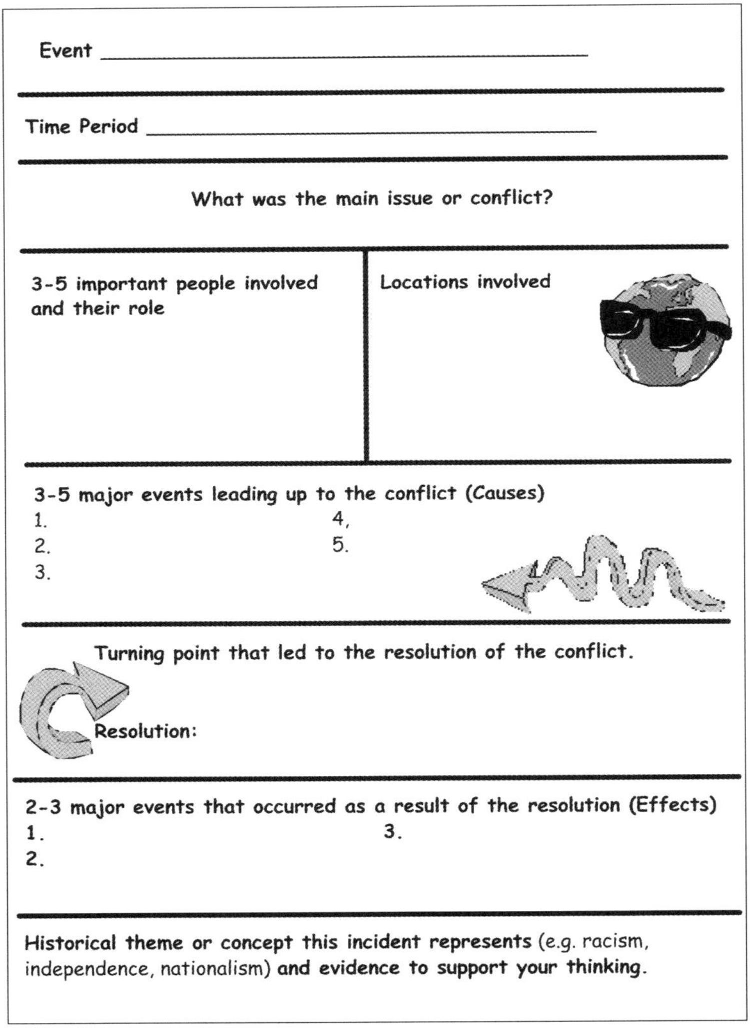

Event _____

Time Period _____

What was the main issue or conflict?

3-5 important people involved and their role	Locations involved

3-5 major events leading up to the conflict (Causes)
1.   4,
2.   5.
3.

Turning point that led to the resolution of the conflict.

Resolution:

2-3 major events that occurred as a result of the resolution (Effects)
1.   3.
2.

Historical **theme** or **concept this incident represents** (e.g. racism, independence, nationalism) **and evidence to support your thinking.**

Title _____

Time Period _____

What was the main issue or conflict?
What type of literary conflict does this represent?

Protagonist (s):	Setting(s)
Antagonist(s)	

3-5 major events leading up to the climax (Rising Action)
1.   4,
2.   5.
3.

Turning point that led to the resolution of the conflict

Resolution (Climax):

2-3 major events that occurred as a result of the resolution
(Denouement)
1.   3.
2.

Literary theme of the narrative and evidence to support your thinking.

- Writing instruction across the curriculum certainly provides tremendous opportunities for teams to be more efficient. Using the same writing process, language, rubrics, and processes benefits students because they receive consistent and straightforward messages about writing. This approach helps teachers when they build on each other's instruction and do not spend time recreating the same wheel. (See Chapter 5.)

- Math often seems to stand alone as a subject area. Other teachers are reluctant to apply math skills in their classes because they feel a bit inadequate or phobic. However, there are a variety of math skills that can be reinforced in social studies and science. Reading all types of graphs is the most obvious way that colleagues can support their favorite math teacher by providing extra practices. Another math skill that can be applied in subjects is choosing the appropriate problem solving approach. "Will making a table or making a drawing or graph help me figure out what's happening in this situation?"

- Every school reform movement in the past 20 years calls for increasing the amount of critical thinking in the curriculum. Teachers revise units to make sure that all elements or levels of Bloom's Taxonomy are present. What doesn't happen enough is the direct teaching of these skills. Teams should divvy up Bloom's and teach students how to analyze, synthesize, and evaluate by modeling and then providing practice of specific strategies. Then in other classes, these skills can be reinforced and reference made to the concrete experience all the students have had. *"Remember when you evaluated the quality of three different cookies in Ms. Jones' class by determining criteria and using a matrix? Well we're going to use that same strategy to evaluate the presidents during Reconstruction."* For good ideas on the direct teaching of higher-level thinking skills, check out the author's other book, *Everyone's Invited! Interactive Strategies that Engage Young Adolescents (NMSA, 2008).*

3 **Bonus Idea - Create fun rituals!** Just like students need to feel valued and psychologically and physically safe in order to learn, team members need to develop healthy, supportive relationships in order to be an effective team. Taking time for humor or celebrating birthdays relieves the accumulation of everyday stress. The late Norman Cousins, a journalist and editor, maintained that 10 minutes of a belly laugh provided him 2 hours of painless sleep while he was fighting a degenerative disease. Another quote to keep in the back of one's mind is "Laughter is a tranquilizer with no side effects," supposedly uttered by one Arnold Glasgow. Developing rituals that celebrate the hard work the team engages in every day and just celebrating one another will help create a productive team. When tension is dissipated, teachers can concentrate on the work at hand and not waste time tiptoeing around each other. Here are some fun things to consider:

- Acknowledge birthdays with a cupcake or card.

- Have lunch together occasionally—everyone brings something for a big salad or just go to the cafeteria together.

- Create special days

    - Every Friday is garlic bagel with veggie cream cheese day.
    - On the 13th of the month everyone wears red.
    - Celebrate often. Commemorate Pi Day, March 14 or World Ocean Day on June 8. Check out the List of Commemorative Days at http://en.wikipedia.org/wiki/List_of_commemorative_days

- Check in with each other. Remembering to poke your head in each morning to say "Yo—how's it going?" is a simple step in building a good relationship with one's teammates.

- Always make sure you have great sub plans on file so that your teammates don't have to generate them as the morning bell is ringing, and the students are stampeding down the hall.

- Commit random acts of kindness:

    - Bring colleagues flowers from your garden.
    - Surprise everyone with a blueberry muffin.
    - Take lunch or bus duty for someone who is under a lot of pressure.
    - Make double chocolate fudge brownies for the team on the day grades are due (add a package of chocolate morsels to a package of a chewy brownie mix).

Next Steps

1 **Teach students appropriate phone, Internet, and e-mail etiquette.** Students are quite capable of scheduling field trips, arranging for guest speakers, and conducting their own research using the phone, Skype, and e-mail. In *Student-Oriented Curriculum*, Wally Alexander reports that sixth graders learned how to schedule their own field trips and contact people to come in and speak to their class. Although they had some false starts, with practice they became proficient. Giving students this type of responsibility serves several purposes. First, it eventually will save time for teachers as students take over the role of scheduler. Second, it gives students practice in using Standard English in a variety of contexts. One of the eight skills that Ruby Payne maintains is essential to teach under-resourced learners is to properly use formal register of language. Modeling and coaching from teachers helps students practice proper syntax, sophisticated vocabulary, and decision making about when to use formal language and when they can be more casual. Resources include:

- TeacherVision (www.teachervision.fen.com): phone and e-mail etiquette for younger students but applicable to middle school students with a few adjustments.

- Investintech (www.investintech.com/content/internetetiquette): a variety of articles on Internet etiquette.

- Mountain State Centers for Independent Living (http://mtstcil.org/skills/manners-2.html): telephone manners.

- Lesson Planet (www.lessonplanet.com): the search engine for teachers.

2 **Use flexible scheduling and team teaching to address cross-discipline standards.** Collaborating to help students meet standards is a good example of working smarter. Manipulating the team schedule for this purpose is one approach. Think of the block of time that the team has with students as a magical giant canvas that can be cut one way on Monday and then reassembled on Tuesday and Wednesday for the regular rotation of classes. Then on

Thursday, it is cut up in a different way to meet the needs of a particular group of students, On Friday it becomes the rotation of classes that shows up on the main office computer.

Figure 11-4. Example of flexible team schedule

Monday	Tuesday/ Wednesday	Thursday	Friday
Period 1: Allied Arts	Period 1: Allied Arts	Period 1: Allied Arts	Period 1: Allied Arts
Period 2 & half of period 3: Team meeting with guest speaker	Period 2: Regular classes	Period 2: Team writing lab to master the "Science Lab"	Period 2: Regular classes
Last half of period 3 and all of four: divided in half for two classes.	Period 3: Regular classes	Period 3: becomes Period 2	Period 3: Regular classes
	Period 4: Regular classes	Period 4: Becomes Period 3	Period 4: Regular classes
Period 5: Lunch & Phys Ed and Health	Period 5: Lunch & Phys Ed and Health	Period 5: Lunch & Phys Ed and Health	Period 5: Lunch & Phys Ed and Health
Period 6 & 7: Regular classes	Period 6: Regular classes	Period 6: Regular classes	Period 6: Regular classes
	Period 7: Regular classes	Period 7: Regular classes	

The schedule doesn't have to change every day or even every week, but it is certainly a mistake to leave it the same and negate a major reason for having a team. The team should control the schedule for learning purposes. The schedule should not be so restrictive that teams cannot manipulate class periods in order to meet learning goals or plan special events. Teams do have to be aware of the needs of special education students and others who are sometimes pulled out of classes. Grousing that pullouts are restrictive won't win the team any friends. A better approach is to invite the pullout teachers to participate in the team activity by suggesting ways the identified students will benefit from the activity and what role the pullout teacher might play. Below are a couple of interesting ways to manipulate the team schedule to meet specific learning goals.

- Build in workshop or lab time (writing, research, real-world math or science). Let's use writing as an example. Every two weeks set aside a chunk of time as a writing lab. Perhaps the science teacher orchestrates workshop/lab time to really hit home on how to prepare a good science lab report. She prepares mini lessons that her colleagues can use in their homerooms. Students are given work time and all of the teams' teachers are circulating and coaching students. Bringing in all the extra help possible—special ed folks, librarian, parent volunteers—reduces the student-teacher ratio so that students receive needed support or individual instruction. Imagine if 75-80 percent of the students master the science lab in that one extended session. The science teacher does not have to re-teach yet again the components of the lab write-up in regular class but can concentrate on supporting the smaller number of students who need extra help during homeroom or study halls. The other teachers benefit because students have had a common experience that includes organization, using technical language, and using evidence to support conclusions—all writing skills the teachers can build on in their own content areas. The next workshop/lab block might focus on math journals and the one after that might focus on open-ended responses for the state test.

- Focus Days: Use team data to identify specific skill deficits of the students. Craft a day around teaching and reinforcing one or two of these skills through various learning styles and multiple intelligences, and give the day a clever name— *The Day of the Infamous Inference! Outwitting Internet Skullduggery! Spotlight: The Big Idea and Its Supporting Details.* The captivating titles and advertising send the message that this day will be different and important. There are a couple of ways to approach such a day. Each content teacher could address the focus skill(s) in his or her regular class, or the team might develop a multi-faceted lesson that everyone teaches with homeroom or advisory groups. Another approach might be to regroup students for the day by the level of their mastery of the skill. Those students who are advanced could work together using more complex material while other students are grouped according to their need. It's critical that the focus skills be applied back in the classrooms over the next few weeks. Lessons in isolation rarely work; there needs to be application of the skill in multiple settings. A Focus Day might also include an hour or so of time to catch students up with missing work. Those students who don't need the extra time can engage in an enrichment activity.

- Extend the invitation of flexible scheduling to colleagues in the allied arts. Perhaps a rocket launching or incredible machine demonstration might extend into the team's schedule of classes so that all of the students could share in the event. This type of extension would also lead to making concrete connections in concepts, skills, and problem-solving approaches across a wider variety of subjects. Also, team teachers would see their students in a different environment and gain additional insight into the whole child. There are always barriers to this type of activity, and everyone will have to use ingenuity to figure out the details. However, making the effort will go a long way in breaking down the "we and them" attitudes that so often arise between the teams and the allied arts teachers.

3 **Incorporate student self-assessment procedures into the team routine.** Team teachers spend a lot of time explaining and justifying student grades to both parents and their students. To decrease time spent this way and to deflate potential rancor, institute student self-assessment that is shared regularly with parents. Three well-known middle school educators who integrated self-assessment into their regular class routines are Wally Alexander, Ross Burkhardt, and Mark Springer. Each has written at least one book detailing their entire approach to teaching, and these descriptions contain specific ideas, strategies, and forms they used to help their students develop responsibility for their own learning.

Check out these exemplary NMSA books written by teachers to learn how they used self-assessment.

Inventing Powerful Pedagogy: Share, 'Steal', Revise, Own. (2009)
by Ross Burkhardt

Soundings: A Democratic Student-Centered Education (2006)
by Mark Springer

Student-Oriented Curriculum (2006)
by Wallace Alexander with Dennis Carr and Kathy McAvoy.

These aspects of self-assessment are critical to include in the process:

- Goal setting: Goals that students set should be very specific accompanied by concrete steps the students will take to meet the goal(s). *I will make sure my finished pieces have correct spelling by using spell check and having an awesome speller teammate help me proofread.*

- Evidence: Students should be expected to gather evidence that demonstrates they are working toward meeting their goal(s) or that they have met the criteria in the assignment rubric. *Please notice that in this essay each of these paragraphs sticks to just one topic, and my writing does not ramble on like it used to.*

- Revisiting and reflecting on goals regularly: Teams need to plan regular times for students to review their goals. Weekly might not be too short a span; if not weekly, then two or three times a quarter. After reflection, students should revise goal(s) and share them with their parents or guardians. *My backpack still swallows my daily math homework. Because keeping it in just one section has not worked very well, maybe I need to get a folder to put my homework in.*

- Academic and learning skills as well as behavior objectives should be included. Academic growth is closely intertwined with behavior, attitude, and "learning to learn" skills. Students need to address all of them. *I will use study hall better this coming week by doing my 20 minutes of independent reading during this time. I will document the pages I read in my daily planner.*

Several of the ideas above are adapted from Lisa Hogan's science teaching at Mt. Ararat Middle School in Topsham, Maine.

Needless to say, students will not automatically or graciously integrate self-assessment into their daily routines. Team teachers must model these strategies and provide scaffolding and practice across the curriculum for students to become adept. Teachers must also hold students accountable in non-confrontational ways. No one really enjoys facing their perceived shortcomings, so students should not see self-assessment as a commentary on their self-worth. Make sure all self-assessments include positive statements. *Conferencing and Reporting* (2004) by Gregory, Cameron, and Davies focuses entirely on ways to help students think about their work in positive ways. The authors provide concrete ideas and formats for ways to use assessment in a variety of settings, including ways to involve parents in the assessment process. Figure 11-5 shows an adaptation of one of their strategies that teams could send home with students.

Figure 11-5. Example of student self-assessment

Update On My Goals for the Home Team!
Date:

My goal(s):

1. To have no more than one or two spelling mistakes in my written work
2. To be able to solve an algebraic equation with one variable

Evidence of my progress:

1. I've stapled work from social studies and language arts. Please notice that there are no red sp's anywhere on them! I caught all of the words I spelled wrong.

2. Watch me solve these two equations for x!

$$3(x+2) + (x-7) = 27 \quad (2y+5) - 10 = 15$$

Comments from my audience:

- **Two compliments I would like to share with you:**
    1. I know spelling is hard for you, and I'm impressed that you have found ways to double-check your work.
    2. I was impressed on how quickly you could solve those equations.
- **One hope I have:**

    That you will continue to take pride in your written work and keep spelling mistakes to a bare minimum.

When parents are part of the process, there are fewer surprises when the report cards come out. Time can be spent working with students and parents to identify specific steps students can take to help them meet the standards and then develop plans of action to support these steps rather than justifying a grade in a heated discussion.When parents are part of the process, there are fewer surprises when the report cards come out. Time can be spent working with students and parents to identify specific steps students can take to help them meet the standards and then develop plans of action to support these steps rather than justifying a grade in a heated discussion.

A last word from Jill...

- Getting more time to address additional responsibilities is out of the question these days, so teams need to figure out smart ways to use the technology they have and not duplicate their efforts. Some of the Web 2.0 tools seem to be just right for teams to use.

- Everyone should to be ecologically smart and eliminate as much paper from team business and classrooms as possible. (*Every year* Americans throw away enough office and writing paper to build a 12-foot wall that stretches from New York City to California, NRDC). Teams need to set a good example for their students.

- With too many standards to address and assess, team teachers need to find those standards that are similar among their various subjects, so they can collaborate in meeting them. Some authors like Janet Hurt (2003) have identified national standards that cross the disciplines. She calls them "umbrella concepts". Her list includes systems, relationships, change, patterns, elements, independence, dependence, processes, structure, order, connections, and cycles. Teams can experiment with an obvious one such as structure— cells have structures; so do short stories and governments—and look for ways teams can save instructional time by helping each other build students' understanding of this concept. That's working smarter.

- Teaming provides flexibility. Flexibility allows teachers to work in different ways to meet student needs when more conventional approaches produce less-than-desired results. Stepping out of traditional mind-sets about time, curriculum organization, and the use of technology may feel uncomfortable, but it is liberating and opens up all sorts of possibilities for teaching and learning. As the Nike commercial says, "Just do it!"

12

Reaffirm Teaming and Its Power

Who knows what middle grades schools will look like in another 40 or 50 years? Teaming certainly has the attributes of an initiative with staying power.

What the Future May Hold

It's the holiday season in 2046 at the Bowman Senior Citizen Complex overlooking Casco Bay, and the staff and residents are looking forward to a visit by local middle grades students for a concert. Some attend the middle school down the road, while other students will join digitally from their island, rural, or very distant homes. No strangers to the residents, students pop in and out regularly in person or over the Internet to conduct interviews for class projects, receive tutoring, participate in book clubs, and play in a community band. Many of the residents are former teachers who still maintain their enthusiasm for being around young adolescents, even though many have been featured on the long-running Today show for reaching their 100th birthdays.

Kendall, a bouncy 12-year-old, is explaining to a small group of the residents how the concert will "happen." Technology will allow the voices and holograph images of their teammates in Japan, New Zealand, and Cameroon to be present at the same time as the students who are at the senior complex in person. The concert will be performed by the Web's blending the voices of both the local students and their distant classmates. Shaking their heads in amazement, the former teachers remember the filmstrips that went "beep" to indicate it was time to advance the frame that were the height of technology when they started teaching. They are also intrigued with the global teams that exist in middle schools today. At the end of their careers they were just beginning to break down classroom walls via Skype conversations with experts around the world. But now, using the Web to be present in classes, students and teachers from all over the world are part of middle grades teams for at least part of the day.

Gloria and Grant chat with Andy about the Pjebscot Team's latest activities. "We're exploring global warming trends and effects, and we're going to present our findings on the local impact to the environmental regulatory groups in our towns." explains Andy. "Our team will be reporting out in five different locations across the globe! We're pretty excited about that and nervous." Grant, a former science teacher, just chuckles to himself and thinks about how long that issue has been under discussion.

"On Friday we are going to have a full day to explore the cultural similarities and differences among all of our teammates. We're going to be in our advisory groups. I'm really looking forward to the cooking part—each different ethnic group will model via the Web how to cook a favorite dish, and the others will follow the directions back in their own location. We'll be eating all day!"

Jill whispered to her former teammates Betty and Peg, "Isn't it just wonderful that an idea from our youth, teaming, has lasted all of these years, proving what we always knew—it rocks!

I hope readers will indulge me as I slip back into the first person of the Introduction that opens this book. It is July in 2010 as I am getting close to finishing work on *Teaming Rocks!* I was reading an ASCD news brief on a new report entitled, *Team Up for 21st Century Teaching and Learning* published by the National Commission on Teaching and America's Future. Trying to practice what I preach about digital literacy, I immediately wanted to check the credentials of this organization I had never heard of before spending any time with the report. Names like Richard Riley, Linda Darling-Hammond, James Comer, Mary Futrell, and Reg Weaver popped up, so I felt confident this was an informed group. Because the title *Team Up for 21st Century Teaching and Learning* immediately intrigued me, I read on. The report focus is revealed by its subtitle, "What Research and Practice Reveal about Professional Learning." As I read the synthesis of the research I found that the teaming referred to was "professional learning communities". I chuckled because the first time I ever heard that term, I said to myself, "Duh—middle schools already have PLCs with their teams." I've had spirited discussions with colleagues who maintain PLCs are totally different from an interdisciplinary team.

But that had not been my experience for the most part. Teams I had been on had similar goals to PLCs': improve student learning and achievement by collaborating to deliver an intellectually challenging curriculum; improve our own practice; and problem solve issues that impacted student learning. The work of traditional PLCs certainly could inform a team's efforts to be become more effective, however, middle grades schools with interdisciplinary and allied arts teams already have the organization to build on as the whole staff works toward becoming an active and vital learning community.

My point in discussing this report is not to debate the issue I outlined above. Rather it is, in closing, to look at middle grades teams through the lens of this report to seek additional support for teaming and to gain insights about improving team effectiveness. Two statements early in the "Synthesis of the Research Findings" jumped out at me:

> *The era of isolated teachers, working alone to meet the myriad needs of all their students, is neither educationally effective nor economically viable in the 21st century.*

> *Just giving today's students a better factory-era school, with teachers delivering text-based instruction in stand-alone classrooms won't prepare them for the 21st century* (p. 3).

Despite a lot of pushback and obstructive behavior from colleagues and policy makers, progressive middle level educators have been trying to find viable ways to address the issues presented in these quotes for 30 years. Interdisciplinary teams that actively collaborate on curriculum and instruction have been one of the major components of this effort. So it was really good to read, once again, that collaboration and curriculum beyond the textbook are critical to creating effective learning environments for students.

Another finding popped out at me that validated my experiences across the years. Again the report is referring to PLCs, however, I think the findings hold true for any type of team, including a middle grades team.

> *The authors also discuss the different perceptions of teachers in both weak and strong communities, and conclude that teachers in weak communities prefer isolation to poor support of their fellow community members, while teachers*

in strong communities tend to feel that they have the power to help every student achieve because they are empowered by the knowledge and support of their colleagues (p.4).

It is not fun being a part of a dysfunctional team. Furthermore, students suffer when their teachers are at odds and send different messages in each class. Teaming is hard work that must be continuous in its attention to team dynamics and philosophy. Chapters 1 and 2 emphasize that working as a team is as much about the teachers building a sense of community and trust among themselves as it is about building community among their students. In almost every chapter I talk about working together to support each other's academic goals. In a perfect middle grades world, professional development time each year would be spent in developing and renewing team norms, working conditions, and goals. But the pressures are great for work on various district initiatives, and the nurturing of teams is rarely on anyone's radar. It often becomes incumbent upon the teams to opt to build positive and dynamic working relationships. And, yes, it may need to happen outside the contract day, and, no, you probably won't get paid for your efforts. I write these words as a lifelong union member; my experience has taught me that extra effort to add value to my job and working conditions has immense paybacks that can't be measured in dollars and cents.

There was one more finding that I just loved to read. "Indeed, those teachers reporting more teacher collaboration in their schools taught in schools with higher student scores on standardized tests" (p. 4). Mertens and Flowers reported in 2003 that teaming (collaboration) was a major factor in improving student learning. The major theme of *Teaming Rocks!* is that collaboration among middle grades team members will lead to increased student learning. I know there will be readers who say I am comparing apples and oranges, but I would reply that collaboration is collaboration no matter which organizational label is applied. Furthermore, teachers that meet daily during a common planning time are in the best position to assess student progress, problem solve issues, and implement innovative solutions. Teaming done well simply works.

Team Up for 21st Century Teaching and Learning outlines six principles that need to be in place if collaborative teams are to be successful (pp. 5-6). They certainly apply to middle grades teams.

1. Shared values and goals
2. Collective responsibility
3. Authentic assessment
4. Self-directed reflections
5. Stable settings
6. Strong leadership support

Principles 1-4 are reflected in this book's chapters, so I will use them as lead-ins for a quick summary of the Big Ideas that wend their way through *Teaming Rocks!* Principles 5 and 6 are not particularly addressed because my purpose is to suggest possibilities for team collaboration not to describe ways to establish and provide on-going support for teams. However, as the reader might imagine, I have opinions on these two principles and will share them briefly.

Principle 1: Shared vision and goals. The report defines this principle in terms of common beliefs about students and teaching and identifying a problem to work on that will lead to increased student learning. Stating that there should be high expectations for all students receives a lot of lip service these days; drilling down to explore our real beliefs about this topic does not. It is an uncomfortable conversation to have, and not everyone wants to share publicly what he or she believes about teaching and learning. However, teams need to continually explore their core values surrounding teaching and learning and find a starting place to set a common goal. Working together on a common goal, no matter how small, is a first step in building the professional relationships necessary to be an effective and efficient team.

Principle 2: Collective responsibility. "Team members should have shared and appropriately differentiated responsibilities based on their experience and knowledge levels" is one of the descriptors of this principle. A major benefit for middle grades teachers and their students is that, on any given team, teachers bring diverse strengths and knowledge to the table. Because I know a lot about the research process but struggle with framing provocative questions that excite and engage students, I can help the team set up a systematic way to address research, plus I can pick my colleagues' brains about ways to improve my questioning techniques. Professional development when it's needed in real time—that's what common planning time provides for the professional learning community called a middle grades team.

Principle 3: Authentic assessment. Teachers view assessments that give them good feedback in a timely manner as valuable because they help the teachers respond quickly to student needs, according to the report. Dylan Wiliam's minute-to-minute and day-to-day approach to formative assessment helps middle grades teachers make decisions about their individual instructional plan—do I need to reteach or can I go on? When information related to the skills and knowledge that cut across the curriculum is shared in common planning time, a team is in position to have a powerful impact on student learning by providing multiple experiences that scaffold and reinforce new learning. Effective teams look at data together and quickly decide on a coordinated response to student learning needs.

Principle 4: Self-directed reflections. "Teams should establish a feedback loop of goal-setting, planning, standards, and evaluation driven by the needs of both teachers and students." When the everyday business of school gets rolling, it is so easy to skip the reflective piece of teaching and learning both in common planning time and the classroom. As things pile up, and we fall behind, we just delete the time set aside to think about how a lesson went or whether a team plan is having any effect or whether or not students can explain why they were successful in a particular task so that they can transfer their actions to another setting. Reflection and metacognition (thinking about our thinking) are major steps in the learning process. When we leave out this step, we as educators are doomed to repeat ineffective strategies and techniques, and students never learn that they have a lot of control over their efforts to be successful in their endeavors. It's important to safeguard this time in the classroom, common planning time, and staff development days.

Principle 5: Stable settings. The report simply says that dysfunctional schools keep teams from functioning well; time and a place to meet and positive administrative support are necessary. Effective teams provide a safe and supportive environment for students and help keep a school from becoming dysfunctional. To be effective, teams require common planning time four times a week, a home space, the freedom to make decisions such as adjusting the team schedule to meet a specific learning need, and an administration that shares common goals with them. In a middle school, strong teams will provide the stability needed for its students to learn and achieve at high levels.

Principle 6: Strong leadership support. Strong support has several elements: creating a physically and intellectually safe school culture, allowing teams to make necessary decisions to support student needs, and stating clear expectations for team performance. Middle grades leadership plays a huge role in the success of the school's teams. While some teams just seem to naturally evolve into effective mini-organizations, most need help. Team building ought to be part of every year's professional development, and team leaders need opportunities to develop their leadership capacity. A team leader often feels like she is walking a tightrope because of the necessity of balancing personal friendships of colleagues with professional responsibilities of leading a team, and sometimes those two come in conflict. But first and foremost, everyone in the school needs to be part of setting the school's goals and sharing the responsibility for helping them come to fruition. A strong leadership team is critical for all of the pieces to come together; a principal cannot lead a school alone. These six principles are useful criteria for any school, no matter its type, to use as a self-assessment of their teams.

Much of the current literature on school reform is in alignment with middle level philosophy as described in documents like *This We Believe, Turning Points, Breaking Ranks in the Middle* and by middle level writers such as John Lounsbury, Paul George, Nancy Doda, Jim Beane, Barbara Brodhagen, and Patti Kinney. Evidently we've been on the right track for 30 years. However, it is imperative to keep moving forward as new challenges arise. Patterns, strategies, and approaches must continue to evolve, making it important to read closely reports such as *Team Up for 21st Century Teaching and Learning*. We need to view these reports not as an additional layer to implement but rather as a fresh lens to view our best practices, so we can continue to refine them to become more responsive to ever-changing student needs. Teaming, the most powerful middle grades practice for meeting student needs, will also continue to evolve. However, some things about teaming should never change: a small, shared group of students; a goal of academic success for each child; common planning time used for curriculum and instruction design; a dedication to the whole child, not just her cognitive needs; and a commitment to make learning engaging, energetic, intellectually challenging, developmentally appropriate, and fun. I would like to leave you with a favorite quote:

> *The tough problem is not in identifying winners; it is in making winners out of ordinary people. That is, after all, is the overarching purpose of education.*
>
> K. Patricia Cross, *Phi Delta Kappan*, 1984

Teams who collaborate help ordinary kids become winners!

Appendix A
Student-Centered Unit Planning

First set your time frame for the unit. Carve two 100-minute blocks of time out of the schedule each week. Or, perhaps the team would prefer using a concentrated amount of time like the two full days right before vacation. Remember that there is no rule set in concrete for the length of a unit—it can last one day or an entire marking period. Then decide the best way to involve students in the planning. The familiar KWL with an extension works well in cases where the teachers choose the overall theme or topic. The format for this planning scenario is an extended KWL chart and is shown below.

What did we learn from the video?	What else do we know to be true about this topic?	What do we wonder about this topic? What questions do we have?	Here's what we found out.

1. Select two or three themes or broad topics. Pick ones that your students can easily relate to their lives outside of school–popular media, music, racism, conflict, the environment, life and death struggles, becoming independent, etc. After students fully discuss these possibilities, they vote by secret ballot for their choice of a preferred theme.

2. With student input identify skills or standards to address in the unit. They might be persuasive writing, practice with graphs and charts, or map reading.

3. Bring the team together in a room in which they can sit in small groups—either on the floor or at tables. Be sure there is wiggle room so that they won't feel like sardines in a can.

4. Announce the top vote getter. Make a show of it with drum rolls, music, or noisemakers.

5. Explain the purpose of the meeting—to plan the unit.

6. Show a short, high-interest video on the topic using a movie clip, TV show, YouTube video or other Internet resource. If you Google "video clips," you will have a multitude of resources from which to choose. Give the students a purpose for watching, such as identifying major concerns, characteristics, or important events. In lieu of a video, the team can create and act out a scenario that would set the stage for the unit. Providing a visual stimulus rather than a reading will catch students' interest because they live in a media-rich world of sounds and images.

7. At the end of the clip, ask students to jot down what they found interesting, things they wondered about, and things they thought might be incorrect or that they didn't believe.

8. Have individuals share with their small groups and make charts that list common ideas that came up. Then have groups share with the whole team. Create Chart #1—What We Learned From the Video!

9. Ask students for things they wondered about or didn't quite believe. Ask them to put these statements into question form. Model the process. Record these questions on Chart #3—Questions We Still Have About This Topic.

10. Have groups make a chart of what else they know about the topic. When they are finished, ask them to take a second look and star those items they are absolutely sure are accurate.

11. Start Chart #2—What Else We Know to Be True About This Topic. Record student responses. It is almost certain something will come up that is not accurate. The facilitator has to bite his tongue at this point and not make the correction. When the chart is complete, ask students if they have any doubts about this information. Those

items challenged need to be written over on the question chart. At this point if incorrect information has not been challenged, it's OK for the facilitator to raise a challenge and rewrite the information as a question on Chart #3. It's important not to give a right answer, but rather let it stand as a question. The students need to do the research to verify information, not just sit and listen to the teacher.

12. The entire group looks over the questions and identifies similar ones to group together. For example, if the video was a clip from a movie about South Africa and Nelson Mandela, questions about apartheid might be grouped together:

- Did the other countries in Africa have apartheid?

- Was apartheid worse than the ghettos in U.S. cities?

- Does something like apartheid exist anywhere today?

13. With the students' full involvement develop broad questions that incorporate the questions grouped together. This task will not be easy for the students and will take some modeling and coaching.

14. Explain to the entire team that the work to answer the team's questions for the most part will take place in their individual classes. However, there is one more remaining task for the team as a whole. Explain that there are some "bottom lines" that have to be incorporated into the unit. Identify these skills/standards and ask the students to review the big questions and chat in their groups about ways to address those skills within the process of answering the questions. Again, modeling an example will help them come up with ideas. For example, to practice persuasive writing, *we could role play people of different races or people from different countries who write letters to the editor of The New York Times about the boycott of South Africa during apartheid.*

15. Teachers should offer for possible inclusion into the unit some of the ideas they had already generated.

16. Students work to answer the unit questions in their classes within the designated time frame following ways and using resources they identified.

17. To close out, plan a major sharing process that includes creating a huge Chart #4—This Is What We Learned! and invite guests to be part of the audience. Allow students to reflect on what they learned and the process they used. Celebrate the effort put forth by the students. Videotape this event and download it to a computer. Ask a couple of students to use a movie making program like iMovie to turn the video into a movie, and then burn a CD for each student with the movie on it. They have a demonstration of their learning to take home and share with their families.

During the unit, team teachers hold the students to the same standards of behavior and quality of work as at any other time. They also might consider collecting relevant data—How's the absentee rate during the unit? Are discipline issues the same? Is work completion improved? Is there any difference in the quality of the work students produce? All of this information is helpful when the team evaluates how well the unit went and whether or not they would invest the energy to plan with students in the future. Collecting varied data turns the unit into an Action Research Project and provides the team with quantitative information to use in future curriculum planning.

Including students in the unit planning process develops their feeling of efficacy. This sense of involvement and personal empowerment is often the first step in helping students take responsibility for their own learning.

Appendix B
Real World Learning Applications and Resources

RWL Component
Learning By Doing

Classroom Application
- Readers/Writers Workshop
- Kinesthetic strategies
- Science labs
- Role playing
- Job shadowing
- Project Based Learning
- Cooperative learning

Resources Organized by Topic

Sites with many resources and ideas
Family Education: www.familyeducation.com/home

Edutopia: www.edutopia.org

Readers/Writers Workshop
In the Middle by Nancie Atwell (Heinemann)

Cooperative Learning:
http://edtech.kennesaw.edu/intech/cooperativelearning.htm

www.co-operation.org

Productive Group Work by Frey, Fisher, and Everlove

Role playing
http://serc.carleton.edu/introgeo/roleplaying

RWL Component

Student Voice and Choice

Classroom Application

- Multiple products to demonstrate learning
- Multiple resources on the same topic
- Planning curriculum with students
- Peer editing
- Publishing for an authentic audience
- Generating student questions to help direct the learning

Resources Organized by Topic

Multiple products

Rubrics for many different products:
http://rubistar.4teachers.org

Universal design: www.cast.org/research/udl/index.html

Using Student Questions in Planning Curriculum

Soundings: A Democratic Student-Centered Education by Mark Springer (NMSA)

Student-Oriented Curriculum by Wallace Alexander (NMSA)

Publishing for an authentic audience

Voice Thread: http://voicethread.com/#home

www.educationworld.com/a_tech/tech/tech042.shtml

RWL Component

Higher Order Thinking

Classroom Application

- Using metaphors
- Project Based Learning
- Using Essential Questions
- Inquiry approach to learning
- Webquests

Resources Organized by Topic

Metaphoric Thinking

Metaphors & Analogies: Power Tools for Teaching Any Subject by Rick Wormeli (Stenhouse)

Synectics: www.writedesignonline.com/organizers/synectics.html

Essential Questions

http://questioning.org/mar05/essential.html

Inquiry, Project Based Learning

www.edutopia.org/project-learning

DeBono's 6 Hats: www.learnerslink.com/posters.htm

Webquests
http://webquest.org/index.php

RWL Component

Real World Connections

Classroom Application

- Problem-Based Learning—solving real problems in the community
- Connecting with experts in the field
- Creating scenarios in the classroom that model real life situations
- Service Learning

Resources Organized by Topic

Problem-Based Learning

http://realworldlearning.pbworks.com/RWL+Resources

http://pbln.imsa.edu/

Connecting with experts

www.edutopia.org/connecting-experts-real-world

Service learning

www.servicelearning.org

www.kidsconsortium.org

RWL Component

Technology

Classroom Application

- Web 2.0 tools like wikis, blogs, slide shows
- Applets (math & science)
- Graphic design
- PowerPoint/Keynote
- 1 to 1 digital learning with either laptops or hand-held devices
- Digital photography
- Digital communication
- Digital probes
- Digital Story Telling

Resources Organized by Topic

Web-based resources and tools

http://PBWorks.com (wiki)

http://wordpress.org (blog)

www.edinformatics.com/il/il_math.htm (math applets)

http://edu.glogster.com (digital posters)

http://animoto.com (easy, free video production)

http://xtranormal.com (text to movie production)

Digital story telling

http://digitalstorytelling.coe.uh.edu

www.storycenter.org

www.jasonohler.com/index.cfm

Apple Learning Interchange

http://edcommunity.apple.com/ali

Microsoft classroom resources

www.microsoft.com/education/default.mspx

One to one computing

www.mcmel.org/web/Doing_1to1_Right!.html

References

ACT. (2009). *The forgotten middle: Ensuring that all students are on target for college and career readiness before high school.* Iowa City, IA: Author.

Aiken, W. (1932). *Adventure in American education Volume I: The story of the eight-year study.* Retrieved from www.8yearstudy.org

Alexander, W., Carr, D., & McAvoy, K. (2006). *Student-oriented curriculum: A remarkable journey of discovery.* Westerville, OH: National Middle School Association.

Allen, J. (1999). *Words, words, words: Teaching vocabulary in grades 4–12.* York, ME: Stenhouse.

Anderman, L., & Midgley, C. (1999). Motivation and middle school students. *ERIC Digest.* Retrieved from www.ericdigests.org/1999-1/motivation.html

Asaro, Jeri. (2010). Tips–Great active learning strategies. *Inspiring Teachers.* Retrieved from http://tinyurl.com/activelearning123

Balfanz, R. (2009). *Putting middle grades students on the graduation path: A policy and practice brief.* Westerville, OH: National Middle School Association.

Beane, J., & Apple, M. (2007). *Democratic schools.* Portsmouth, NH: Heinemann.

Beard, C. (2009). *Jurassic park: The webquest.* Retrieved from http://fayette.k12.in.us/~cbeard/jp/webquest.html

Beck, I. (2007, November). *Rev up instruction in the middle grades.* Presentation at the annual conference of the National Middle School Association, Houston, TX.

Beck, I., McKeown, M., & Kucan, L. (2002). *Robust vocabulary instruction: Bringing words to life.* New York: Guilford Press.

Ben Johnson. (2010, January 9). Liven up your lessons with choice [Web log post]. Retrieved from www.edutopia.org/lesson-engagement-student-choice

Berckemeyer, J. (2009). *Managing the madness: A practical guide to middle grades classrooms*. Westerville, OH: National Middle School Association.

Berger, E. (2010, July). TV Interview with Rob Caldwell on *207 Bill Green's Main*. Channel 6, Portland, ME. Retrieved from www.wcsh6.com/life/programming/local/207/story.aspx?storyid=119537&catid=50.

Berkowitz, R., & Eisenberg, M. (Creators). Introducing the big 6 [Web page]. Retrieved from www.big6.com/kids

Berry, A., & Wintle, S. (2009). *Using laptops to facilitate middle school science learning: The results of hard fun*. Gorham, ME: Center for Education Policy, Applied Research, and Evaluation. Retrieved from http://usm.maine.edu/cepare

Black, P., & Wiliam, D. (1998). *Inside the black box: Raising standards through classroom assessment*. London: Kings College London School of Education.

Blakemore, S.J., & Choudhury, S. (2006). Development of the adolescent brain: Implications for executive function and social cognition. *Journal of Child Psychology and Psychiatry, 47*(3), 296–312. Retrieved from www.paed.uni-muenchen.de/~epp/nil/nil/pdf/BlaChoJCPP_06.pd

Bransford, J., Brown, A., & Cocking, R. (Eds.). (2000). *How people learn: Brain, mind, experience, and school*. Washington, DC: National Academy Press.

Brazee, E., & Capelluti, J. (1995). *Dissolving boundaries toward an integrative curriculum*. Westerville, OH: National Middle School Association.

Burkhardt, R. (2009). *Inventing powerful pedagogy: Share.'Steal.' Revise. Own*. Westerville, OH: National Middle School Association.

Burris, C. C., Wiley, E., Welner, K. G., & Murphy, J. (2008). Accountability, rigor, and detracking: Achievement effects of embracing a challenging curriculum as a universal good for all students. *Teachers College Record, 110*(3), 571–608. Retrieved from http://tinyurl.com/3y2uzz2

Butler, D.A., & Liner, T. (1996). Whole language on a team. In T. Dickinson & T. Erb (Eds.), *We gain more than we give: Teaming in the middle school* (pp. 465–485). Westerville, OH: National Middle School Association.

Carr, D. (2003). *Getting started with curriculum integration*. Topsfield, MA: New England League of Middle Schools.

Carroll, T., Fulton, K., & Doerr, H. (Eds.). (2010). *Team up for 21st century teaching and learning: What research and practice reveal about professional learning*. Retrieved from the National Commission on Teaching and America's Future at www.nctaf.org/TeamUp.html

CAST. (2010). What Is Universal Design? Retrieved from www.cast.org/research/udl/index.html

Chase, M., Mullins, D., & Sferes, T. (2009, October). *Imagine being... The kindest middle school in Maine*. Workshop presentation at the annual conference of the Maine Association for Middle Level Education, Carrabassett Valley, ME.

Collins, J. (2001). *Good to great: Why some companies make the leap... and others don't*. New York: HarperCollins.

Davies, A. (1998, November). *Classroom assessment*. Presentation at the conference "Standards-based Local Assessment System that Promotes Student Success" sponsored by Professional Development Center, University of Southern Maine and Assessment Institute of Portland, OR, in Augusta, ME.

Doda, N., & Thompson, S. (Eds.). (2002). *Transforming ourselves, transforming schools: Middle school change*. Westerville, OH: National Middle School Association.

Dyck, B. (2010). Making meaning of personal learning networks. *Middle Ground, 13*(3), 33.

Feinstein, S. (2004). *Secrets of the teenage brain: Research-based strategies for reaching and teaching today's adolescents*. San Diego, CA: The Brain Store.

Field Guide for Change Agents. (2010). [Slideshow]. Retrieved from www.slideshare.net/bhazzard/field-guide-for-change-agents

Flowers, N., Mertens, S., & Mulhall, P., with Krawczyk, T. (2007). *Applying current middle grades research to improve classrooms and schools*. Westerville, OH: National Middle School Association.

Frey, N., & Fisher, D. (2008). *Teaching visual literacy: Using comic books, graphic novels, anime, cartoons, and more to develop comprehension and thinking skills*. Thousand Oakes, CA: Corwin Press.

Frey, N., Fisher, D., & Everlove, S. (2009). *Productive group work: How to engage students, build teamwork, and promote understanding*. Alexandria, VA: Association for Supervision and Curriculum Development.

Gardner, Traci. (2010). Inquiry on the Internet: Evaluating web pages for a class collection. *ReadWriteThink*. Retrieved from the IRA/NCTE website at http://tinyurl.com/evaluation123

George, P., & Lounsbury, J. (2000). *Making big schools feel small: Multiage grouping, looping, and schools-within-a school*. Westerville, OH: National Middle School Association.

Gorlick, A. (2009). Media multitaskers pay mental price, Stanford study shows. *Stanford News*. Retrieved from http://news.stanford.edu/news/2009/august24/multitask-research-study-082409.html

Gregory, G., & Kuzmich, L. (2005). *Differentiated literacy strategies for student growth and development in grades 7–12*. Thousand Oakes, CA: Corwin Press.

Gregory, K., Cameron, C., & Davies, A. (2004). *Conferencing and reporting*. Merville, BC, Canada: Connections Publishing.

Group think. (n.d.) [Web page]. Retrieved from website of Psychologists for Social Responsibility at www.psysr.org/about/pubs_resources/groupthink%20overview.htm

Hoerr, J. (1989). The payoff from teamwork. *Business Week*, July 10. 56–62.

Hurt, J. (2003). *Taming standards: A commonsense approach to higher student achievement, K–12*. Portsmouth, NH: Heinemann.

Inquiry-based learning. (n.d.). *Worksheet Library*. Retrieved from www.worksheetlibrary.com/teachingtips/inquiry.html

IRA issues RTI guideline. (2010). *Reading Today, 27*(4), 1–7.

Ivey, B. (2008). Classrooms without borders: Students teaching students. *Middle Ground, 12*(1), 22–23.

Jackson, A., & Davis, G. (2000). *Turning points 2000: Educating adolescents in the 21st century*. New York & Westerville, OH: Teachers College Press & National Middle School Association.

Kist, W. (2010). *The socially networked classroom*. Thousand Oakes, CA: Corwin Press.

Knowlton, D., & Wielgus, M. (Summer 2005). Using asynchronous discussion to support middle school philosophy and concept. *Meridian Middle School Computer Technologies Journal, 8*(2).

Kriete, R. (2002). Morning meeting: An overview. *The Morning Meeting Book* [Online Book Chapter]. Retrieved from www.responsiveclassroom.org

Kristof, N. (2008, November 16). Talia for president [Electronic version]. *The New York Times*. Retrieved from www.nytimes.com/2008/11/16/opinion/16kristof.html?_r=3

Kuntz, S. (2005). *The story of Alpha: A multiage, student-centered team—33 years and counting*. Westerville, OH: National Middle School Association.

Kuzmich, L. (2007). *Research-based vocabulary strategies*. Presentation at the Promising Futures Literacy Academy at Colby College, Waterville, ME.

Leahy, S., Lyon, C., Thompson, M., & Wilian, D. (2005). Classroom assessment: Minute by minute, day by day. *Educational Leadership, 63*(3), 19–24.

Levy, S. (2008). The power of audience [Electronic version]. *Education Leadership, 66*(3), 75–79.

Lewis, B. (2008). *The teen guide to global action: How to connect with others (near & far) to create social change*. Minneapolis: Free Spirit.

Lipton, L., & Wellman, B. (2000). *Pathways to understandings: Practices in the learning-focused classroom*. Sherman, CT: Miravia.

MacIver, D. (1990, February). Meeting the needs of young adolescents. *Phi Delta Kappan, 71*(6), 458–464.

Maine Center for Meaningful Engaged Learning. (n. d.). Meaningful engaged learning. Retrieved from www.mcmel.org/web/Meaningful_Engaged_Learning.html

Maine Center for Meaningful Engaged Learning. (n. d.). Real world learning. Retrieved from www.mcmel.org/web/Real_World_Learning.html

Marzano, R. (2004). *Building background information for academic achievement: Research on what works in schools*. Alexandria, VA: Association for Supervision and Curriculum Development.

Marzano, R. (2009). Six steps to better vocabulary understanding. *Educational Leadership, 67*, 83–84.

Marzano, R., Pickering, D., & Pollock, J. (2001). *Classroom instruction that works: Research-based strategies for increasing student achievement*. Alexandria, VA: Association for Supervision and Curriculum Development.

Marzano, R. J., & Kendall. J. S. (1998). *Awash in a sea of standards*. Aurora, CO: Mid-continent Research for Education and Learning.

Master list of team building games. (n.d.). [Web page]. Retrieved from International Association of Teamwork facilitators www.teachmeteamwork.com/teachmeteamwork/master_games_list

McKenzie, J. (2005, March). Essential questions. *The Question Mark, 1*(5). Retrieved from http://tinyurl.com/questions125

Mertens, S. B., & Anfara, V. A., Jr. (2006). *Research summary: Student achievement and the middle school concept.* Retrieved from www.nmsa. org/ResearchSummaries/StudentAchievement/tabid/276/Default.aspx

Mertens, S., & Flowers, N. (2003). Middle school practices improve student achievement in high poverty school. *Middle School Journal, 35*(1), 33–43.

Most dropouts leave school due to boredom, lack of encouragement. (2006). Retrieved from *Philanthropy News Digest* at http://foundationcenter.org

National Association of Secondary School Principals. (2006). *Breaking ranks in the middle: Strategies for leading middle level reform.* Reston, VA: Author.

National education technology standards. *International Society for Technology in Education.* Retrieved from www.iste.org

National Middle School Association. (2010). *This we believe: Keys to educating young adolescents.* Westerville, OH: National Middle School Association.

National Resources Defense Council and Health Schools Network. (n.d.). Fact sheet: Saving paper in schools.[Web page]. Retrieved from www.nrdc.org/ greensquad/library/paper.html

NCREL/The Mitiri Group. (n.d.). What's so different about the 21st century? [Web page] Retrieved from Retrieved from www.metiri.com/features.html

Nesin, G., & Lounsbury, J. (1991). *Curriculum integration: Twenty questions— with answers.* Atlanta, GA: Georgia Middle School Association.

New Study Finds Time Spent Online Important for Teen Development. (2008, November). John D. and Catherine T. MacArthur Foundation. Retrieved from www.macfound.org/site/apps/nlnet/content2.aspx?c=lkLXJ8MQKrH &b=2024163&ct=6355221&notoc=1

Norman Cousins. Retrieved from *Wikipedia* at http://en.wikipedia.org/wiki/ Norman_Cousins.

November Learning. (2009). Information literacy resources. Retrieved from http://novemberlearning.com/resources/information-literacy-resources

Palfrey, J., & Gasser, U. (2008). *Born digital: Understanding the first generation of digital natives.* New York: Basic Books.

Payne, R. (2008). *Under-resourced learners: 8 strategies to boost student achievement.* Highlands, TX: aha! Process.

Pink, D. (2009, November). *A whole new mind*. Keynote address at annual conference of National Middle School Association, Indianapolis, IN.

Prof Heppell's dead Weblog. (January 29, 2007). Assessment and new technology: New straightjackets or new opportunities? [Web log post]. Retrieved from www.heppell.net/weblog/stephen

Puentedura, R. (2010, January 21). Images in sequence [Webcast]. Retrieved from http://maine121.org/webcasts/archives

ReadWriteThink. Persuasion map. (2010). Retrieved from http://tinyurl.com/persuasion123

Route 21. (2007). Life and career skills. *Framework for 21st Century Learning*. Retrieved from www.21stcenturyskills.org

Selby, Monte. (2009, November 17). Middle school curriculum. [Electronic mailing list message]. Retrieved from https://mail.google.com/mail/?shva=1#search/19+Nov+2009+to+20+Nov+2009+%28%232009-282%29/12515d0652f67661

Sousa, D. (2006). *How the brain learns* (3rd ed.). Thousand Oaks, CA: Corwin Press.

Spencer, J. (2009). *Everyone's invited! Interactive strategies that engage young adolescents*. Westerville, OH: National Middle School Association.

Spencer, J., & Toy, C. (2010, January 5). Curriculum and instruction. *Bright Futures Webcast #2*. Archived at www.maine.gov/education/ml/dev.html

Sprenger, M. (2009). Focusing the digital brain. *Educational leadership, 67*(1), pp. 34–39.

Sprenger, M. (2005). *How to teach students to remember*. Alexandria, VA: Association for Supervision and Curriculum Development.

Springer, M. (2006). *Soundings: A democratic student-centered education*. Westerville, OH: National Middle School Association.

Springer, M. (1994). *Watershed: A successful voyage into integrative learning*. Westerville, OH: National Middle School Association.

Stars and constellations project [Web page]. *Electronic emissary*. http://tinyurl.com/experts123

Teachers see their work as "calling" study suggests. (2000). Retrieved from http://archives.cnn.com/2000/US/05/24/new.teachers.study/

Tomlinson, C. A. (2010). One kid at a time. *Educational leadership, 67*(5), 12–16.

Vacca, R., & Vacca, J. (1989). *Content area reading* (3rd ed). Glenview, IL: Scott Foresman.

Van Hoose, J., Strahan, D., & L'Esperance, M. (2001). *Promoting harmony: Young adolescent development and school practices.* Westerville, OH: National Middle School Association.

Vatterott, C. (2009). *Rethinking homework: Best practices that support diverse needs.* Alexandria, VA: Association for Supervision and Curriculum Development.

Welcome to Route 21. (2007). Retrieved from *The Partnership for 21st Century Skills* www.p21.org/index.php?option=com_content&task=view&id=266&Itemid=120

Wiggins, G. (2007, November). What is an essential question? *Big Ideas Education e-journal.* Retrieved March 18, 2010, from http://tinyurl.com/questions123

Wiliam, D. (2007). *Ahead of the curve: The power of assessment to transform teaching and learning.* Bloomington, IN: Solution Tree.

Wiliam, D. (2006, December). *Using assessment to support learning: Why, what, how?* Presentation for the Maine Department of Education, Portland, ME. PowerPoint retrieved from www.maine.gov/education/presentations/dylanwiliam122006.ppt

Williams, T., & Kirst, M. (2010, March 4). Gaining ground in the middle grades: Lessons from California. *Education Week.* Retrieved from www.edweek.org

Willingham, D. (2009). *Teaching content is teaching reading.* Retrieved archived video from www.danielwillingham.com

Wood, J. (2000, July/August). Innovative teachers hindered by the "Green-eyed Monster." *Harvard Education Letter.* Retrieved from www.hepg.org/hel/article/138

Wormeli, R. (2010). Honor roll? Really? *Middle Ground, 13*(3), 31.

Zike, D. (2002). *Reading and study skills: Foldables–high school.* New York: Glencoe.

Zike, D. (2007). What is a graphic organizer? [Web page]. Retrieved from www.dinah.com/manipulatives.php

National Middle School Association

Since 1973, National Middle School Association (NMSA) has been the voice for those committed to the education and well-being of young adolescents and is the only national association dedicated exclusively to middle level youth.

NMSA's members are principals, teachers, central office personnel, professors, college students, parents, community leaders, and educational consultants in the United States, Canada, and 46 other countries. A major advocacy effort is Month of the Young Adolescent. This October celebration engages a wide range of organizations to help schools, families, and communities celebrate and honor young adolescents for their contributions to society.

NMSA offers publications, professional development services, and events for middle level educators seeking to improve the education and overall development of 10- to 15-year-olds. In addition to the highly acclaimed *Middle School Journal*, *Middle Ground* magazine, and *Research in Middle Level Education Online*, we publish more than 100 books on every facet of middle level education. Our landmark position paper, *This We Believe*, is recognized as the premier statement outlining the vision of middle level education.

Membership is open to anyone committed to the education of young adolescents. Visit www.nmsa.org or call 1-800-528-NMSA for more information.